Whaat does the LORD your God require of you, but to fear the LORD your God, to walk in all His ways and to love Him, to serve the LORD your God with all your heart and with all your soul, and to keep the commandments of the LORD?

DEUTERONOMY 10:12-13 NKJV

THE 100
MOST IMPORTANT
BIBLE VERSES
FOR MEN

Presented to:

_____

Presented by:

_____

Date:

_____

Those who wait on the Lord shall renew their strength; they shall mount up with wings like eagles, they shall run and not be weary, they shall walk and not faint.

Isaiah 40:31 nkjv

THE 100
MOST IMPORTANT
BIBLE VERSES
FOR MEN

W PUBLISHING GROUP
A Division of Thomas Nelson Publishers
Since 1798

www.wpublishinggroup.com

The 100 Most Important Bible Verses for Men
© 2006 by GRQ, Inc.
Brentwood, Tennessee

Published by W Publishing Group, a Division of Thomas Nelson, Inc., P.O. Box 141000, Nashville, Tennessee 37214.

Managing Editor: Lila Empson
Associate Editor: Laura Kendall
Manuscript: Robin Schmitt
Design: Thatcher Design, Nashville, Tennessee

Library of Congress Cataloging-in-Publication Data

100 most important Bible verses for men.
       p. cm.
ISBN 0-8499-0032-8
1. Christian men—Religious life. 2. Christian life—Biblical teaching. 3. Bible—Quotations. I. Title: One hundred most important Bible verses for men. II. W Publishing Group.
BV4528.2.A15 2006
220.5, 2—dc22

                              2005022271

Printed in China
06 07 08 09   9 8 7 6 5 4 3 2

It is better to be patient than powerful; it is better to have self-control than to conquer a city.

PROVERBS 16:32 NLT

Contents

Every part of Scripture is God-breathed and useful one way or another—showing us truth, exposing our rebellion, correcting our mistakes, training us to live God's way. Through the Word we are put together and shaped up for the tasks God has for us.

2 TIMOTHY 3:16–17 MSG

Introduction

The Bible is the most powerful book ever written, and a man can learn valuable lessons from considering its most significant verses. Each devotion in *The 100 Most Important Bible Verses for Men* illuminates a key passage from the Bible, highlighting the truth it contains and clearly showing how that truth relates to your life. Some of the verses may be familiar to you, such as the golden rule, John 3:16, or the Ten Commandments, while many others will represent hidden gems whose wisdom will benefit you immensely.

Every verse in the Bible is a window into the whole of God's truth. As you contemplate each vital principle in the following pages, you'll gain a comprehensive view of who God is and what life with him is all about. These one hundred verses and their accompanying devotions will give you insight into what the Bible really means—inspiring you to pick up the Bible itself and read every last verse it contains.

The 100 Most Important Bible Verses for Men will teach you about God and about yourself. Every one of these verses offers a core concept that will help you become the man God wants you to be. They will open your eyes to what true manhood is and empower you to achieve it. As only the words of the Bible can, they will generate in you a strong passion for God, a deep love for others, an unshakable inner peace, and an indescribable joy.

He who has seen Me has seen the Father.

God and Man

Jesus was a man, just like you. He was born, grew up, learned how to make a living, and worked for a number of years. He got hungry and ate, got thirsty and drank, got tired and slept. He traveled around, made friends, and eventually made his mark on the world. When he died, he was buried just like any other man.

But this ordinary guy made a very important claim: that he was God in person, that anyone who observed him would know what God is like. He backed up this claim as well, per-

12   THE 100 MOST IMPORTANT BIBLE VERSES FOR MEN

forming miracles with the power of God, teaching with the wisdom of God, reaching out to outcasts with the compassion of God, and forgiving people's wrongs with the authority of God.

Jesus was a man, and yet when he commanded a storm to cease, the wind and the waves complied. He was a human being, and yet when he spoke to the mob who came to arrest him, the entire throng fell to the ground. Jesus was made of flesh

> **Jesus can completely relate to you, because he is every bit a man.**

and blood, and yet on the third day after they laid his body in a tomb, he walked right back out. Jesus can completely relate to you, because he is every bit a man. He can also teach you a lot about God, as he is every bit God himself. Simply watch what he does and listen to what he says.

Jesus's life was well documented; the New Testament in the Bible chronicles his words and his actions. Make a commitment to learn all you can about him, so you'll begin to understand God.

E̲very promise of the L**ord** your God has come true. Not a single one has failed!

J**oshua** 23:14 **nlt**

Signed Contract

When a man signs a contract, he literally puts his name on the line. He makes a written vow to perform in some manner, perhaps to deliver goods or services or pay for them. As he conscientiously follows through on his obligation, he establishes good credit and goodwill. People trust him and want to continue doing business with him.

God put his pledges in writing. He was willing to risk his reputation, which he highly values, by having his promises recorded in the pages of the Bible. They're right there in black and white for every man to see. God has already fulfilled many of them, and the details of how he did so have been similarly recorded. He certainly wouldn't mind if you checked it all out for yourself.

One thing about God is, he never changes. If your examination of his "credit history" indicates a pattern of promises made and promises kept, you can be sure he will remain reliable. Then you can focus on his promises to you. Many of the pledges that God made to individuals long ago have implications for you today, but some were limited to a specific person, time, and place. It's important not only to know what God's promises to you are but also to understand them well. Once you do, you'll find they're almost too good to be true. Yet don't forget who signed his name under each one.

> **Many of the pledges that God made to individuals long ago have implications for you today.**

God is always willing to do business with a man willing to deal with him. Learn all you can about the great promises he offers you, and determine to take him up on each one. (See Matthew 5:3–10; Proverbs 3:5–6; Jeremiah 17:7–8; Deuteronomy 31:8; Psalm 128:1–4.)

W**atch therefore, for you do not know what hour your Lord is coming.**

Matthew 24:42 nkjv

Never Mind When

If you hear a weather prediction or an economic forecast, you understand implicitly that despite all the knowledge and technology used to formulate it, ultimately it's just somebody's best guess about the future. That's never the case with a prophecy from God. Anytime a spokesperson he has chosen makes a proclamation, you can bet the farm that it's not a matter of *if* it will come to pass but *when*.

Take a look at the prophecies in the Bible that have already come true. The Bible is largely a collection of history books written at different times by various authors, and it's amazing to read a declaration from God in one of its books and then see the statement proved correct hundred of years later in another. When you realize how many fulfilled prophecies there are in the Bible, you'll gain a genuine respect for the accuracy of God's projections, and learn to seriously consider his outlook for the days ahead.

> **The most significant prediction in the Bible is Jesus's promise that he will come back.**

The most significant prediction in the Bible is Jesus's promise that he will come back. And the most important thing he said about this event is that even though it's only a matter of time before it happens, you shouldn't focus on the when. Instead, a loyal follower of Jesus will always be "watching," looking out for Jesus's return and looking after all God has entrusted to him until the day Jesus sets foot on earth again. God will reward such a man well for his faithfulness.

~ oﬀ⊙

Obey Jesus attentively every moment until he comes again, however long that may take. Make waiting for his return a time of joyful anticipation, free from guilt and full of hope.

G od has chosen you and made you his holy people. He loves you. So always do these things: Show mercy to others, be kind, humble, gentle, and patient.

COLOSSIANS 3:12 NCV

Nice Guys

Men today are striving to reclaim their manhood; they're trying to learn what it means to be strong, to be assertive, to be a man according to God's standards. They no longer want to be thought of simply as nice guys. But in this admirable search for authentic masculinity, there's a danger that men will abandon the quieter virtues of manhood for those that are more dramatic.

God *is* calling you to be a real man. He has singled you out because he loves you, and he will teach you how to become a man in every sense. That's partly why he sent Jesus into the world: to provide you with a model of perfect manliness. Jesus was the greatest man who ever lived. There was a fathomless strength to his character. He was bold enough to criticize influential people, and force-ful enough to drive away everyone who was using God's temple as a mar-ketplace. But he was more than simply a powerful guy. He was also a man who was warm-hearted and sympathetic, never hesitant to show his soft, caring side.

> **God designed you to be a nice guy.**

If you're going to be a true man, you will need all the virtues God intended men to possess. God designed you to be a nice guy. He meant for you to have a kindly quality about you, undergirded by the inner strength and drive to fulfill all of his purposes for your life.

Work hard to acquire every virtue of authentic masculinity. It may seem like trying to move in several directions at once, but God will make it possible for you to attain all these attributes.

Those who worship hollow gods,
god-frauds, walk away from their only
true love. But I'm worshiping you, God,
calling out in thanksgiving!

JONAH 2:8–9 MSG

Man's Greatest Love

The only true love a man has ever known—love that is pure, unconditional, steadfast, and everlasting—has come from God. He has loved you longer and stronger than anyone has, more than your parents, your friends, your wife, your children, or anybody else. God's love has been coming your way since before you were conceived, and regardless of how you've responded to him or what kinds of decisions you've made over the years, it has never let up for an instant.

However, God has felt the pain of separation every time you've been distracted from him by the people and things in your life. Any father would suffer greatly if his son poured all his affection into sports and school and friends and music and movies and computers and video games. All these are fine

> The greatest love a man will ever experience is the bond between himself and God.

with a father—until they interfere with his relationship with his son. That is of utmost importance to him.

The greatest love a man will ever experience is the bond between himself and God. When you honor God's perfect love for you by putting your relationship with him above all else and revering him alone, your connection with him will remain strong. You'll find that the love you share with God is more exciting, vital, and fulfilling than anything else in your life. Your relationships with others will thrive because of it, and you'll enjoy all of God's gifts to you with deep gratitude and delight.

~*

Are you communicating with God in prayer regularly? Do you find that you're increasingly aware of his presence each day? These are the surest signs that you are being true to your greatest love.

"You shall love the LORD your God with all your heart, with all your soul, with all your mind, and with all your strength." This is the first commandment.

MARK 12:30 NKJV

Life's Focus

Can you imagine what it would be like to work on a carving like Mount Rushmore? Suspended high on the face of a cliff, you'd have to keep the big picture in perspective while chipping away at the rock inches in front of you. Somehow you'd have to focus on two things at once: what you're doing at the moment, and ultimately why you're doing it.

That's not much different from a man's everyday life. Each day presents a mountain of ways to expend your passion, time, and energy, and you have to determine where you're going to chisel. The decision is much easier when you can see the big picture clearly and understand what matters most in life. That will help you set your priorities straight.

Jesus knew that life's most important purpose is to love God, and that's where he concentrated his effort. By following Jesus's example, you'll make

> **By following Jesus's example, you'll make the right choices.**

the right choices. Your life will take on a shape that exhibits your love for God, and it will stand forever as a monument to him.

Did you know that in the game of chess, all the pieces have a numerical value except the king? That's because he's invaluable. Every other piece has its function and worth, but falls into its respective rank after him. The king is the whole object of the game, and a wise player keeps him in focus at all times. Make God your highest priority, and all the other areas of your life will fall nicely into place.

If you are searching for meaning in your life, invite God into it and make him your focal point. Give God top priority, because he gives everything else purpose.

What does the LORD your God require of you, but to fear the LORD your God, to walk in all His ways and to love Him, to serve the LORD your God with all your heart and with all your soul, and to keep the commandments of the LORD?

DEUTERONOMY 10:12–13 NKJV

Job Description

When a man is charged with a responsibility, he needs to know exactly what's expected of him. A man hired by a corporation receives a written job description, a breakdown of the job's component tasks. Much of the Bible is devoted to clarifying God's two most important commandments: to love him and to love others. It's easy to go through the Bible and create a checklist you can use to ensure you're achieving these two main goals. God doesn't leave you to your own devices to figure out how to fulfill life's most crucial obligations; he spells everything out plainly.

The checklist Moses gave the Israelites just before they entered the Promised Land is the perfect place to begin yours. Moses reminded the people that living with God meant utterly respecting him, doing things his way, adoring and worshiping him, working to achieve his purposes, and obeying him. Elsewhere in the Bible are God's instructions to be honorable and fair, merciful and compassionate, humble and faithful, and to always acknowledge that he is God.

> **God doesn't leave you to your own devices to figure out how to fulfill life's most crucial obligations; he spells everything out plainly.**

God puts these duties at the top of his job description for you. They are much more significant to him than other actions such as giving away money or going without food for a time. These things are still on the checklist, but sacrifice means so much more when your everyday behavior reveals your love for God and others.

Review God's job description for you and commit yourself to fulfilling it. Use his checklist every day to help you meet the two overarching responsibilities in every man's life: loving God and loving others.

25

Accept each other just as Christ has accept you.

ROMANS 15:7 NLT

Join the Club

Jesus had a reputation for being a "friend of sinners." He was perfectly willing to hang around with people who were less than perfect. It's a good thing he was, because according to the Bible, every man falls into that category. However, the Bible also says that people carry the imprint of God in their very being. Jesus was able to look beyond everyone's defects and recognize their basic humanity. He never prejudged or stereotyped people, but rather approached them as individuals who were worthy of dignity and respect just because God made them and loved them.

There's a lot of truth to the saying "Nobody's perfect." Jesus, being God, is the only exception to that rule. He is also the only person in a position to judge anyone. He reached out to you, *knowing* you were truly beneath him, so it's essential that you extend your hand to those you only *think* aren't as good as you.

> **Jesus was able to look beyond everyone's defects and recognize their basic humanity.**

Remember what it cost God to embrace you as a friend. Since God is absolutely perfect, the only way he could have a relationship with you was to find a way to get rid of all your imperfections. He accomplished that through Jesus's death on the cross. If God sacrificed so much to welcome you into his presence, why not give up a little pride and be willing to associate with all of his children? They may seem flawed, but the cross offers hope that God will one day make them perfect.

Start making an effort to befriend people whom others have rejected. You'll soon have quite a rep yourself—as a man who is just like Jesus. That's the best reputation you could ever earn.

No eye has seen, no ear has heard, and no mind has imagined what God has prepared for those who love him.

1 CORINTHIANS 2:9 NLT

An Inconceivable Eternity

After reading the apostle Paul's words regarding how little any man knows about the future God has planned, what do you think the chances are that your concept of heaven is accurate? Take a moment to think about how you envision the next life, and where that mental image originated. What is it based on—a movie you saw, some popular notion about the hereafter, or perhaps your own imagination? However you picture heaven, and wherever you picked up the idea, it's important to recognize that most likely it's way off the mark.

Always remember that heaven is beyond anything a man can comprehend, because if you forget this truth, you're bound to settle on a view of eternity that falls far, far short of reality. Guys can get bored with their own vision of paradise.

If heaven is merely some kind of retirement community where all men do is fish or play golf all the time and talk about their glory days back on earth, why not just stick around here where you can find a few more thrills?

> **If your concept of paradise doesn't raise your pulse, chuck it out the window and start thinking outside the box.**

One glimpse into the real heaven would set any man's heart racing. If your concept of paradise doesn't raise your pulse, chuck it out the window and start thinking outside the box. Not to replace it with another image that is just as inaccurate, but to begin contemplating how magnificent an eternity with God will be, because the essence of heaven is the inconceivable joy of his presence.

Jesus knew about heaven firsthand, and he was willing to die so you could experience it too. Does your level of excitement about heaven reflect the price Jesus paid to get you there?

${}^{\text{I}}$ am He who lives, and was dead, and behold, I am alive forevermore. Amen. And I have the keys of Hades and of Death.

REVELATION 1:18 NKJV

Jailbreak

Hell is the exact opposite of heaven—its essence is God's absence. It's completely void of both God and goodness. In the book of Revelation, the apostle John described it as the "second death." At the first death a man's spirit leaves his body; if he suffers the second death, his spirit is separated forever from God and from everyone with God in heaven. Hell is much like a prison in which a man sentenced to life without parole is permanently cut off from society.

To keep you out of this prison, Jesus went there instead. On the cross, he died not only physically but also spiritually—that is, he was separated from God. Completely innocent, he voluntarily entered the prison in your place, and then he burst out, taking the keys from the warden in the process. Jesus's triumphant declaration means you don't have to fear death.

> Jesus has always possessed eternal life, an extraordinarily powerful kind of life that lasts forever.

Jesus was the "Living One" long before his victory over death and hell. Like his Father, who is frequently called the "living God" in the Bible, Jesus has always possessed eternal life, an extraordinarily powerful kind of life that lasts forever. It could never have been taken away from him, but he gave it up willingly for one reason: to share it with you. Thanks to Jesus, you can escape the fate of hell and have the same amazing kind of life he has.

Jesus is equal to God, and he holds the power of life and death in his hands. Does the way you're living your life show him the gratitude and respect he deserves?

No one who trusts God like this—heart and soul—will ever regret it.

ROMANS 10:11 MSG

No Regrets

If you're like most men, you want to live life with no regrets. When you reach the end of the line, you want to be able to look back and feel that you've experienced life fully, that you haven't missed out on anything. In the final analysis, you want to feel that you haven't made any big mistakes you could have avoided. You want to believe that you've made the best of your opportunities in life.

The Bible says that if you put your complete confidence in God, trusting him fully in every area of your life and taking him at his word for all your needs, you'll never be sorry. You won't spend your final hours on earth wishing you would've put a little more faith in other things, such as money. Just the opposite. You'll reflect on your life and real-ize it was rich in a way you never dreamed possible, and that believing in God's promises was the best deci-sion you ever could have made.

> **It's not too late to shift your confidence to where it needs to be today.**

No matter how much time you have left in this world, it's imperative to choose right now where to stake your future. You may have some regrets from misplacing your trust in the past, but it's not too late to shift your confidence to where it needs to be today. If you pick wisely and through prayer commit yourself totally into God's hands, you'll have every reason to celebrate your choice from now until the end of your life.

If you haven't trusted God before or have trusted him only a little, begin putting *all* your faith in him today. It's an entirely different way to live—yet there's no better way to go.

Without faith it is impossible to please Him, for he who comes to God must believe that He is, and that He is a rewarder of those who diligently seek Him.

The Key to It All

There's a reason why the words *LORD* and *GOD* often appear in capital letters in the Bible. Modern translations of the Bible use these words to indicate where the actual name of God is found in the original manuscripts. Ancient scribes used a special font when they hand-copied this name onto their parchments. In the Dead Sea Scrolls, for instance, God's name stands out from the rest of the text, just as on the pages of a Bible. It was the name God told Moses at the

34   THE 100 MOST IMPORTANT BIBLE VERSES FOR MEN

burning bush, and it was considered so holy that for a long time people were afraid to say it aloud. Today no one is certain how it was pronounced. Its meaning, however, is very clear: God's name is "I AM."

The essence of faith is taking God at his word. Faith at its root is a man's agreeing with God, accepting that what he says is true. It begins with

> **Trusting God is the key to every man's relationship with him.**

God's name, which addresses the core issue of whether or not "he is." With all the science and technology available in the twenty-first century, there's still no way to prove or disprove God's existence. You must rely on his word.

Trusting God is the key to every man's relationship with him. It's the crucial element in knowing him and earning his favor. God declares he is real. If you believe this and everything else he says, and search for him wholeheartedly, you'll be lavishly compensated: you'll find him, and all his promises will bear your name.

The commonsense approach to life is to first see proof, then believe. But above all, God wants every man to trust him. Believe God's words; he will prove himself to you and reward your faith.

What does the LORD your God
require of you, but to fear the
LORD your God, to walk in all
His ways and to love Him, to
serve the LORD your God with
all your heart and with all your
soul, and to keep the commandments of the LORD?

DEUTERONOMY 10:12–13 NKJV

You can't worship God and Money both.

Matthew 6:24 MSG

Got to Choose

By and large, today's money is nothing more than bits of electronic data stored in some computer somewhere. If the computer at your bank finds the right sequence of bits for your account, it will approve a purchase. Scrooge McDuck would get quite a jolt if he tried to wallow in that kind of currency. If you find you're putting more thought and energy into building up your bank accounts than cultivating your relationship with God, take a moment and think about exactly what you're dedicating your life to.

Nobody loves money for what it is; a man loves money for what it can do. Money represents purchasing power, the power to buy whatever you want to buy, go wherever you want to go, and do whatever you want to do. So the hard truth is that worshiping and serving money equates to living for yourself rather than for God. Fortunately, there's a way out of that trap, by making God your Master and money your servant.

> **Nobody loves money for what it is; a man loves money for what it can do.**

Money has many honorable functions in the life of a man who's wholeheartedly committed to God. It enables you to purchase the things you and your family need, as well as supply other people's needs through charitable giving. If you submit yourself to God and gain control over your budget, money can free up your schedule so you'll have more time for him and others. Choose the right master, and your life will truly be enriched.

Men are great at compartmentalizing their lives, but God and money require different approaches. Instead of trying to juggle them separately, focus on God and let him teach you how to handle your finances.

Do to others what you would want them to do to you.

LUKE 6:31 NCV

Golden Oldie

Many men are familiar with the golden rule yet misinterpret it, like a guy who hums his favorite song for years without really understanding the lyrics. You might think this rule is a formula for changing how others act toward you, but Jesus never implied that if you deal with people fairly, they'll reciprocate. He was talking about how to respond when others treat you poorly in the first place. His point was that you should always treat people well—not because you expect them to return the favor but because it's the right thing to do.

Have you ever noticed litter on the golf course as you pulled up to one of the tees? Following the golden rule is like making the trip to the trash can regardless of whether you think the foursome behind you will bother, simply because you know that's how God would like everyone to take care of his creation. It's how you'd want others to care for your property.

> **The immense value in the golden rule lies in Jesus's promise of great reward for choosing to live God's way no matter what other guys do.**

This rule is a biggie. It reflects God's second most important commandment, after loving him, and that's to love others the way you love yourself. Jesus's famous principle shouldn't be considered golden because it has magical powers to make people behave more decently toward you. In fact, Jesus expressly stated that you shouldn't expect your good deeds to be repaid. The immense value in the golden rule lies in Jesus's promise of great reward for choosing to live God's way no matter what other guys do.

As a person yourself, you're an expert on how people want to be treated. Apply this expertise to your relationships by always following the golden rule, and show that you also know what pleases God.

Work hard and cheerfully at whatever you do, as though you were working for the Lord rather than for people. Remember that the Lord will give you an inheritance as your reward, and the Master you are serving is Christ.

COLOSSIANS 3:23–24 NLT

Giving Your Best

How would it affect your work if God bought out your company and made himself president? You'd probably be motivated to work more diligently, not so much because God was observing you (though that would be part of the reason), but because you'd be inspired to give him your best effort. You'd want to do your highest-quality work, certain that your job was important to him and helped fulfill his noble purposes. Your attitude toward your work would change as well; you'd labor with an inner joy, knowing that you were an integral member of God's team and that he would honor your contribution someday.

According to the apostle Paul, you need to recognize that God really *is* your boss at the highest level. For all the above reasons, you should be doing your best job at work, right now. God is watching, your job matters greatly to him, you are valued, and one day he will pay you back for everything you've done.

> **If you find it difficult to remember why you're doing what you do, start punching in with God before you punch in at work.**

If you find it difficult to remember why you're doing what you do, start punching in with God before you punch in at work. Use your thirty-minute commute to connect with God, dedicating your workday to him and asking him to help you give him your all. On the way home, ask God to debrief you on how well you served him and show you ways you can improve. Imagine how your career will benefit from such individual time with your highest-ranking boss every day.

～⫯〇

Memorize Paul's words to the Colossians and recall them while you work. Remember that God is your real boss, and you'll be motivated to serve him with greater effort and joy.

We are His workmanship, created in Christ Jesus for good works, which God prepared beforehand that we should walk in them.

EPHESIANS 2:10 NKJV

Positive Energy

Some guys think God takes all the happiness out of life by stamping every wonder he created with an "Off Limits" sign. But living God's way is less about avoiding bad things than it is about doing what's more worthwhile. God's purpose isn't to ruin your fun; it's to add meaning and joy to your existence. If your experience with God has lacked vitality, try shifting your focus off his *don'ts* and onto his *dos*. It'll put wind in your sails.

Every man's goal should be to become what God intends him to be, and to accomplish what God means him to do. These objectives will start your heart pumping, get you out of bed, and get you going. And as God's *dos* (such as his command to serve him wholeheartedly) give you forward momentum, you'll realize that all of his *don'ts* (such as his warning not to make possessions your focus) are meant to keep you from getting bogged down.

> **An ordinary man serving God is extraordinary indeed.**

God may have designed you to be someone great or planned for you to be a regular guy. Becoming the latter may not sound very inspiring, but an ordinary man serving God is extraordinary indeed. God often uses common people to achieve mighty things. The work God has in mind for you may run the gamut from everyday good deeds to outstanding great works. It's all important to God. Any life lived for his purposes is highly significant, and choosing that goal will set your heart on fire.

⁓✧⊙

Find and fulfill your purpose in life by connecting more intimately with Jesus. Build your relationship with him to discover who you are and receive the power to become it.

W̃e do not lose heart. Even though our outward man is perishing, yet the inward man is being renewed day by day.

2 CORINTHIANS 4:16 NKJV

Gray Hairs

Television sitcoms poke a lot of fun at middle-aged guys trying to cling to their youth by coloring their hair, combing over their bald spots, wearing toupees, and tightening their belts. Although these characters are laughable, you have to admire their spunk. Everyone knows they're fighting a losing battle, but their eternal optimism keeps them going.

Thankfully, God offers you a better hope than this. It's true that you're on the same road as every other man physically, whether you're in your prime, just over the hill, or well along in the aging process. But as the apostle Paul reminded the Corinthians, if you invite God's Spirit to live in you, then your inner self—the real you, the part of you that lasts for-ever—will be made brand-new every day of your life. Not only that, but when you allow God into your heart, he will start changing you on the inside, and he will continue to improve you until you join him in heaven, at which point you'll be perfect. Talk about the prime of your life!

> **If you invite God's Spirit to live in you, then your inner self—the real you, the part of you that lasts forever—will be made brand-new every day of your life.**

With God you'll grow older *and* better. You can color your hair if you want to, but God sees gray hair as a crown of honor. Why not wear it proudly? Despite all the emphasis modern culture places on youth, a man whose self-identity and self-esteem are rooted in his relationship with God can choose to age with dignity and grace.

～)))◌

Participate daily in God's renovating work inside you. Allow God to replace your old, wrong patterns of thinking and behaving with right ones, and you'll feel more and more like a new man.

Though you do not see him, you trust him; and even now you are happy with a glorious, inexpressible joy.

1 PETER 1:8 NLT

No Greater Delight

Some events in a man's life evoke feelings of bliss. One is falling in love, winning the heart of the girl you're crazy about. Another is becoming a father, seeing for the first time the child God has given you and falling in love all over again. And then there is achieving a dream, accomplishing the goal you've had your heart set on for years.

If you've known any of these blessings, you have an inkling of the flood of joy that God begins to pour out on a man who decides to follow him. That's because each of these experiences reflects a different quality of the best event that could occur in any man's life—becoming a Christian.

Think of what it means to put your confidence in God. You've never laid eyes on God; no portrait or photograph or even physical description exists. Yet you get to know him, come to adore him, and choose to join your life with his forever. Like falling in love. You realize that this new person in your life is the most awesome, precious gift you've ever received. Like becoming a father. And the longer you walk with God, the more excited and jubilant you feel, because you know you're moving ever closer to a fantastic destination. Like achieving a dream. Recognizing that God brings such enduring, expanding, exhilarating joy is one of the most compelling reasons for a man to believe in him.

> **The longer you walk with God, the more excited and jubilant you feel, because you know you're moving ever closer to a fantastic destination.**

Trust God, allow your spirit to respond joyfully to his presence, and as a blind man learns to use his remaining senses to perceive others, more and more you'll "see" him.

Be filled with the Spirit.

EPHESIANS 5:18 NKJV

Dramatic Lighting

When a man designs and builds a grand house, with an impressive entrance, high ceilings, elaborate stonework, and beautiful hardwood floors, he will invest a lot of thought and effort into lighting. Proper illumination will bring the house to life, accenting its best features and making it both inviting and useful. A good home is filled with light.

The Bible says that every man's body is a place for God's Spirit to reside. God intends for the light of his presence in your life to be much more than a single bulb in the foyer or a night-light in the corner of a bedroom. His plan is for your entire being to be flooded with his brilliance, so that every area of your life is fully illuminated by his love and goodness and truth. Being full of God's Spirit this way bene-fits you directly, and the light of his presence within you overflows to ben-efit those around you.

> God intends for the light of his presence in your life to be much more than a single bulb in the foyer or a night-light in the corner of a bedroom.

In practical terms, being "filled with the Spirit" means giving God's Spirit complete access to your being each morning, inviting him to light up every aspect of your life. When you do this, your mind will be filled with thoughts of God all day, thoughts that bring peace and hope and joy. Your heart will be filled with love for God. And every situation that comes your way you will face with God, illuminated through his wisdom and strengthened through his power.

Ask God to inundate you daily with his Spirit, so that your life shines with all of his wonderful qualities. It's the most enlightened way a man can live.

Put yourself aside, and help others get ahead. Don't be obsessed with getting your own advantage. Forget yourselves long enough to lend a helping hand.

PHILIPPIANS 2:3–4 MSG

Looking Out for Number Two

Everybody wants a better job, a bigger home, a nicer car. Nowadays these things come and go quickly. Employees frequently switch jobs and companies throughout their careers. People live in a house five or six years and then move on. And many cars are driven only a short time before their owners sell them or trade them in. Amid all this upward mobility, God is calling men to a much higher standard of living.

One of the strongest themes in the Bible is the call to look out for the well-being of others. As you tend to your career and your personal affairs, learn to replace selfish ambition with godly ambition.

Other people will soon need your job, your house, and your car. Look out for their interests by being responsible with these things while you possess them, and by showing integrity as you transfer ownership. Take good care of your car and home, keep maintenance records, and be honest and fair when you sell. Likewise, do your job to the best of your ability, keep your files in order,

> **Trust that anytime you're looking out for the other guy, God is looking out for you.**

and train your replacement well, helping to ensure his or her success. One day you may even decide to step aside and let someone else move ahead. Trust that anytime you're looking out for the other guy, God is looking out for you.

Make a commitment to always consider others' welfare as well as—or instead of—your own. Ask God to help you trade your ambition for his, and trust him to look after your well-being.

Delight yourself also in the LORD, and He shall give you the desires of your heart.

PSALM 37:4 NKJV

One Wish That's Guaranteed

God isn't a genie who will grant a man's every whim, yet there is one desire he is always certain to fulfill. Anytime you ask him to give you more of himself, he is happy to oblige. That's because God is a Father who loves to give good gifts to his children, and there is no better gift that he could give you than himself.

A loving father doesn't give his son everything he wants. He gives his son what's best for him, and tries to teach his son to desire only what's best for him. God may give you the things you're longing and praying for, or he may not, depending on how they fit into his plan for your life. Either way, his eye is on a much higher goal: helping you learn to search for happiness in a relationship with him. His focus is there because he knows that no matter how hard you look, he is the only real source of joy you'll ever find.

> **The secret to obtaining your heart's desires is to change the desires of your heart.**

The secret to obtaining your heart's desires is to change the desires of your heart. You have to learn to want what's worth wanting above all else. Choose the one longing that will truly satisfy you. Wealth? Probably not. Health? Yes, but it may not be enough. A strong moral character? Wisdom to make good decisions? Ask God to help you to draw closer to him, to grow more intimate with him, to discover your deepest joy in him. That's one request he will always honor.

What's the core yearning of your heart? To what are you devoting your life? Make God the object of your passion, and he will fulfill your greatest desires.

Blessed are those who mourn, for they shall be comforted.

Matthew 5:4 nkjv

A Consoling Touch

When a man is grieving, he's in a condition to experience God in a way that's not possible otherwise. He can receive something that a person who isn't grieving cannot: God's consoling touch. Everybody deals with sorrow at some point, so eventually every man has the unsought opportunity to encounter God this way and sense the comfort Jesus promised. The important thing to remember during a dark period in your life is that he offered such hope, and you are to trust in his Word and look for God's presence.

Grieving is difficult and painful. When you lose a loved one because of death or a broken relationship, you feel as if something has been torn from inside you, as when a great tree is uprooted from the ground. It's not a desirable state to be in, yet it's a unique condition in which God can do incredible work. The soil is loosened. Your defenses have crumbled, and your focus is shifted away from a man's normal concerns. You have an acute awareness that you're not in control, and a growing realization that you need God. In such an environment God can sow solace, peace, and encouragement.

> **Find some private place where you can weep and voice your feelings to God.**

Don't be afraid to mourn when you suffer an overwhelming loss. Grief brings a wide range of emotions, from sorrow to anger, which men often bottle up inside. Find some private place where you can weep and voice your feelings to God. You'll feel a touch from him you may never have felt before.

Grief can lead to exponential growth in a man's relationship with God. Allow yourself to go through the process, and allow him to help you through it.

Just as rain and snow descend from the skies and don't go back until they've watered the earth, doing their work of making things grow and blossom, producing seed for farmers and food for the hungry, so will the words that come out of my mouth not come back empty-handed. They'll do the work I sent them to do, they'll complete the assignment I gave them.

Isaiah 55:10–11 MSG

A Powerful Speaker

God's intrinsic, unlimited power makes him a forceful speaker—when he talks, things happen. There is no greater evidence of this than his first recorded words: when he said, "Let there be," there was. God's words created the universe, and they can alter a man's life. They are capable of producing dramatic change. God's words can take a passive, timid man and make him assertive and confident and bold.

One reason why God's words are so relevant and full of impact for men today is that they're true. Truth is strong and endures. Many of history's finest orators, such as Abraham Lincoln and Martin Luther King Jr., were such effective speakers because their messages were based on God's truths. Yet there's an even greater dynamic at work when God speaks. God's words conduct his power like high-voltage electric lines. This can be seen in his Son. Jesus is considered one of history's best speak-

> **God's words will do for you what he intends them to do.**

ers, but his ability went far beyond teaching. He told a woman named Martha that anyone who believed in him would live; then with a word he raised her brother.

God's words will do for you what he intends them to do. This will encourage you when the Bible points out work in your heart that needs to be done, work you can't begin to accomplish alone. God's words have the power to effect a man's need for change.

~⁂~

God has lots of confidence in the power of his words. Put them to the test, to see if you can trust as much as he does that they will make you a better man.

If any of you lacks wisdom, let him ask of God, who gives to all liberally and without reproach, and it will be given to him.

JAMES 1:5 NKJV

Greater Perspective

A man living in the information age must be smart enough to recognize that despite the vast amount of knowledge available today, he needs wisdom that the Internet and CNN can't provide. His connection with God is far more valuable and important than his access to cable television and the World Wide Web.

With all the news and information from TV, radio, newspapers, magazines, and the Internet come views and opinions that can influence how a man sees himself and responds to the world around him. The media and the culture have a powerful way of shaping what men believe they should be and do. God knows this makes a man's life confusing, and he is delighted when you come to him for counsel. It's what he wants you to do anytime you need to know how to handle a situation, because nobody has a better perspective on life than he does.

> **The media and the culture have a powerful way of shaping what men believe they should be and do.**

For the most part, God has a "freedom of information" policy when it comes to sharing his wisdom. Aside from a few secret things he has chosen to keep to himself for now, God's wisdom is accessible to every man. A great deal of it has already been published in the Bible, so that's a good place to begin seeking it. And God's Spirit is always ready to advise any man willing to ask him for insight. You just need enough wisdom of your own to turn to God for answers, and to heed the guidance he offers.

—⟋⟍⟍

Get into the habit of going to God for counsel on matters both big and small, and always follow his advice. It's the one way to ensure that you'll live wisely.

We are His workmanship, created in Christ Jesus for good works, which God prepared beforehand that we should walk in them.

EPHESIANS 2:10 NKJV

God . . . has reconciled us to Himself through Jesus Christ, and has given us the ministry of reconciliation.

2 CORINTHIANS 5:18 NKJV

Cease-Fire

When a relationship is broken, rarely is one side fully to blame. Yet that was the case when Adam disobeyed God, destroying his bond with his Creator. God had done no wrong, but he made the first move toward rebuilding his relationship with humankind. In the beginning of the book of Genesis, God laid out a road map to peace that led through the entire Bible. It went by way of his Son's reconciliatory death in the Gospels, and culminated in God's great reunion with man in the book of Revelation.

God has called you to be part of his peace process, by fostering harmony between yourself and others. Adam's mistake shattered his connection with his wife as well as his attachment to God, and ever since there's been division between people. Part of God's purpose for you is to help set things right.

> **God has called you to be part of his peace process, by fostering harmony between yourself and others.**

When you feud with another man, you almost always share part of the blame. That's all the more reason for you to extend your hand in an offer of peace. God makes it your duty to determine your fault in the matter, then own up to it and ask the other guy for forgiveness, expressing a desire to patch things up. That's all you can do, besides praying that God will help the other guy do the right thing as well. But it creates an atmosphere in which wounds can be healed and a relationship restored.

Take the first step toward burying the hatchet. God will help you, because he values relationships highly. Resolve your disputes with others as quickly as you can—it will improve your connection with God.

May our Lord Jesus Christ Himself, and our God and Father, who has loved us and given *us* everlasting consolation and good hope by grace, comfort your hearts and establish you in every good word and work.

2 THESSALONIANS 2:16–17 NKJV

Moral Support

Every man needs encouragement as he tries to live a godly life, especially if he's in an environment that offers little moral support. Perhaps the code of ethics at your workplace falls short of the Bible's standards for integrity. You may notice other employees acting dishonestly; your own boss may ask you to lie to clients to protect the bottom line. God will stand behind you in such a situation, urging you to hold tightly to your convictions.

When you feel as if you're alone on the gridiron in a hostile stadium, surrounded by the other team's colors and by voices of opposition, pray to God for support. He will reassure you of his presence and affirm your desire to do what's right. You'll know in your heart that he is close at hand, and that knowledge will fill you with hope and strength of purpose. It will give you the confidence you need to press on.

> When you feel as if you're alone on the gridiron in a hostile stadium, surrounded by the other team's colors and by voices of opposition, pray to God for support.

God will encourage you in other ways as well. When the prophet Elijah hid in the desert, thinking he was all alone in the world, God told him that in fact there were seven thousand godly people in Israel. God will help you see that you're not alone either. You'll look around the field and discover that you're surrounded by teammates whose hearts beat true.

Strive to live according to God's principles, and look to him for encouragement when it seems you're the only one who does. God will always be there to spur you on.

Fear this glorious and awesome name,
THE LORD YOUR GOD.

DEUTERONOMY 28:58 NKJV

Due Respect

As a man learns about what God is like and about the wonderful things God has done for people through the ages, and as he experiences God more and more in his own life, he will realize that God has earned a spectacular reputation. God has made a name for himself that stands alone. It is distinguished, distinct from every other name. And that's precisely what the Bible means when it describes God's name — and God himself — as *holy*: set apart, unique, exceptional.

God's name has been misused throughout time. Men have degraded it by using it frivolously or, even more inconceivable, invoking it as a curse. Also, many who have claimed to represent God have sullied his good name through words and actions that aren't in line with his character. But God cares a great deal about his reputation and his name, and he will always see to it that they are polished off and reestablished to their proper height, where they reflect the reality of who he is.

> **If you love God, you'll contend for his honor most fiercely of all.**

A man will stand to defend his own reputation, the honor of his family, the name of a close friend. If you love God, you'll contend for his honor most fiercely of all. But before you can do that with integrity, you must be certain that in every way you are revering his name. This involves veneration, esteem, respect, even a healthy sense of fear. God's name is majestic, and it is always to be held in the highest regard.

~⟩⟩⟩○

God promises that if you honor him, he will honor you. Are you upholding his name in everything you think, say, and do? What are some ways you could treat God's name with more respect?

By humility and the fear of the LORD are riches and honor and life.

PROVERBS 22:4 NKJV

Modest Reward

Modesty and a healthy respect for God go hand in hand, because a man gains an accurate estimation of himself the moment he sees himself in proper relation to God. When a man understands how magnificent and wise and powerful God is, and realizes how much he owes God for all the talents, resources, and opportunities God has given him, his attitude toward himself changes. He becomes a humble man, a self-effacing man, a man with a self-image rooted in reality. Ironically, this is the kind of man God holds in high regard and lifts up in the eyes of others.

God has a topsy-turvy effect on both the unassuming and the pretentious. If you were to shake a container of gravel, you might think that the smaller, lighter stones would rise to the top and the bigger, heavier ones would settle to the bottom. But just the opposite happens. God tends to shake up men's lives a lot, and the outcome—though the Bible predicts it—is usually unexpected. God raises modest men, those who are truly big, to heights of esteem and prosperity and fulfillment, while causing boastful, smaller men to stumble.

> God raises modest men, those who are truly big, to heights of esteem and prosperity and fulfillment, while causing boastful, smaller men to stumble.

Giving God the reverence he deserves, and basing your self-image on who he is, will put you in the right position to receive every reward he promises to men who take pride in him rather than themselves. Better yet, seeing yourself in proper relation to God will put your relationship with him right on track.

~⫯⊙

Is your self-image genuinely modest? Does your attitude toward God show deep respect? Humility leads to a rich, satisfying life, earning you God's approval and the esteem of others.

Be careful and guard against all kinds of greed. Life is not measured by how much one owns.

Luke 12:15 ncv

Not Good

Michael Douglas's character in the movie *Wall Street* declared that greed was good. He may have put it a little bluntly, but on some level was he right? As capitalism continues to spread around the world, it's easy to get the impression that life is all about accumulating as much wealth and property as possible. Doing otherwise seems wrong. If a man goes through a time when all he can afford to do is maintain the status quo—he can't buy a new house, remodel his current home, trade in his car, or purchase anything that isn't a necessity—he feels as if his life is going nowhere. And "downsizing" seems downright unnatural.

In today's world the desire to acquire seems acceptable, just part of life. It's time to stop and take another look at this issue. If you really want to know what life is all about, you've got to get God's perspective on things. Only he has a handle on the real facts of life. And the truth is, greed is *not* good. The hunt

> **The hunt for more, more, more is simply not a man's purpose for living.**

for more, more, more is simply not a man's purpose for living. Jesus pointedly asked his listeners what good it would do to gain the whole world yet lose your soul.

God created men to be much more than ruthless tycoons or insatiable consumers. Your life doesn't reside in your bank account or your investments or your belongings; it resides in your relationship with him.

Employ a man's best weapon against greed: giving. Share whatever amount of wealth God has given you with the needy. Instead of unhealthy desire, you'll experience a wholesome sense of peace, well-being, and satisfaction.

Go therefore and make disciples of all the nations, baptizing them in the name of the Father and of the Son and of the Holy Spirit, teaching them to observe all things that I have commanded you; and lo, I am with you always, even to the end of the age.

MATTHEW 28:19–20 NKJV

Mission Statement

Many men attempt to clarify their purpose in life by crafting a personal mission statement. This helps them determine the reason for their existence and focus on fulfilling it. After Jesus died on the cross and rose again—achieving his own purpose on earth, to provide everlasting life for everyone who believes in him—he gave his followers a clear-cut mission statement: to tell everybody in the world what he had done and invite them to follow him.

Every man needs to incorporate into his personal mission statement the essence of Jesus's command, known as the Great Commission. However, the way this will shape each man's life will vary. Adopting the Great Commission inspires some guys to stand on street corners, some to go door-to-door, some to travel to foreign countries. It may motivate you to talk about Jesus with the people you care about most, such as family members, coworkers, and friends.

Doing your part to fulfill the Great Commission involves risk, often to valued relationships. And it means more than just telling people about Jesus and walking away. It's about creating followers of Jesus, and that also requires helping people to make a formal commitment to him and teaching them to obey him. Finally, it's something no

> **Doing your part to fulfill the Great Commission involves risk, often to valued relationships.**

man can do alone. After issuing the Great Commission, Jesus made an equally great promise: to always be with you so you can accomplish it. He will go wherever you go, helping you achieve his final command.

Make it your mission to tell others about who Jesus is, what he did, and what he taught, and to encourage them to follow him. It's one of the most significant purposes of your life.

First cleanse the inside of the cup and dish, that the outside of them may be clean also.

MATTHEW 23:26 NKJV

Inside Out

When a guy pulls out of a car wash and hits the road, other drivers may think he looks pretty spiffy in his shined-up SUV. But only he knows the condition of the interior. Actually, he's only half aware of it; he may recognize that the dash is dusty, but God alone knows everything that's hidden under the seats.

In any issue involving purity, such as how you interact with members of the opposite gender, God is concerned not only with your behavior but also with your heart. When you invite his Spirit into your life, he will do a thorough detailing job on you. Although this process may be difficult and uncomfortable, it's in your best interest to fully cooperate with him. If you allow God's Spirit total access to your inner being, he will help you clean up all your private thoughts and deep-rooted attitudes, and you'll experience a freedom you've never known before.

> **If you allow God's Spirit total access to your inner being, he will help you clean up all your private thoughts and deep-rooted attitudes.**

Your heart is the source of all your behavior. When it's spotless, your conduct is exemplary, and you are pure inside and out. Then God can use you for his most noble purposes. But as you may already know, it's impossible to clean out your heart on your own. The power to purify your inner being comes directly from Jesus's death on the cross, and is given to you by God's Spirit. He will show you everything in your heart that needs to go and enable you to get rid of it.

~〜

Ask God to clean out your heart, and be willing to let go of impure desires no matter how natural and right they seem to you. You'll enjoy the benefits and freedom of purity.

I have filled him with the Spirit of God, in wisdom, in understanding, in knowledge, and in all manner of workmanship.

EXODUS 31:3 NKJV

God-Given Talents

Men display an incredible range of talents. You see this all around—in business, sports, science, medicine, the arts. It's amazing what guys can do. Where does all this ability come from? The Bible says it comes straight from God.

This truth is seen in Bezalel, the man God chose to head construction of the tabernacle, a large tent in which the Israelites could worship God as they crossed the desert. God gave Bezalel extraordinary capability in working with metal, wood, and stone. He was a master craftsman and designer, and he was able to teach others. God empowered

Bezalel for one important reason: to build the structure God envisioned.

Bezalel's story teaches four crucial points. Two are overt, and two lie just below the surface. First, God gives men aptitude and wisdom. Some of it is hard-wired at conception; some is acquired through education and experience. However, God orchestrates the whole process. He makes men and molds them. Second, God not only gives men talents but also gives his Spirit, which "powers up" these talents, lending

> God not only gives men talents but also gives his Spirit, which "powers up" these talents, lending them a supernatural potency.

them a supernatural potency. Third, God has specific intentions when he doles out abilities. They are meant to be used for his lofty purposes. Finally, if God's purposes are to be accomplished, the man receiving these gifts must be willing to use them for God's glory — by doing the work God is calling him to do. If God's tabernacle was to be built, Bezalel had to set hammer to chisel.

God has given you a unique blend of skill, ability, and knowledge. Thank him for all your gifts, ask him to show you their purpose, and be willing to use them to achieve it.

Is there anyplace I can go to avoid your Spirit? To be out of your sight? If I climb to the sky, you're there! If I go underground, you're there! If I flew on morning's wings to the far western horizon, you'd find me in a minute—you're already there waiting!

PSALM 139:7–10 MSG

Universal Coverage

God is omnipresent—he is everywhere all the time. No matter where a man goes, God is with him. Your cell phone company may be good, but it can't guarantee coverage like that. God is always right there beside you. This is true whether or not you sense his presence, just as a strong mobile phone signal in a well-covered area is present regardless of whether or not your cell phone is on.

This fact has two important ramifications for every man. The first is that no matter how hard you try, you can't hide from God. He sees everything you do. Incidentally, he also knows everything you think, so you can't fool him either. The thought of always being clearly in God's view may make you feel uncomfortable and guilty—God often has that effect on men, once they're aware that he really is watching them. If so, your best response is to run toward God. You'll find that he is not only always around but also always willing to forgive.

> **Whenever you pray to God, he is in the right place at the right time to offer encouragement, help, comfort, guidance, and protection.**

The second ramification of God's steadfast presence is that he is always immediately available to you. He hears a man as well as sees him. Whenever you pray to God, he is in the right place at the right time to offer encouragement, help, comfort, guidance, and protection. There is no place in the universe you can go where he can't be there for you.

—

Remind yourself every morning of God's constant nearness. Make your awareness of it a source of joy for you all day long, and allow yourself to bask in his presence.

Godliness with contentment is great gain.

1 Timothy 6:6 NKJV

This Is the Life

Grasping the wisdom of this short verse is like hitting the power button on your remote control in the middle of a sports car commercial. Immediately everything changes. One moment your mind is consumed with the best the world has to offer—beauty, speed, luxury, prestige—the next all is peaceful and quiet. The advertiser's busy, noisy attempts to make you discontented with your life are silenced, and you're free to feel satisfied with all the blessings God has given you.

Understanding the apostle Paul's message to Timothy is vital to living the rich life God intends for you, because it reveals the true meaning of the word *profit*. Every man has a desire to advance, make progress, improve his lot. Madison Avenue offers the world's definition of *achievement*; Paul provides God's. Embrace the latter, and your life will take on new direction. Like a running back reorienting himself in a chaotic play, you'll turn and begin striving for the right goal.

> **Godliness and contentment—that's the goal, men.**

Godliness and contentment—that's the goal, men. Marketing gurus say that if you can acquire it all, you'll be content. The Bible says that if you're godly and content, you already have it all. The clincher, the truly amazing thing about the life God offers, is that even when you have it all, he continues to pour on blessings. Jesus promised that if you make godliness and contentment your aim, your heavenly Father will give you everything you need. That's the abundant life God wants to give you.

Develop godly contentment by focusing on your gratitude for all God's gifts. Ask God to teach you what true contentment is—not complacency but a condition of the heart that motivates you toward great deeds.

As far as the east is from the west, so far has He removed our transgressions from us.

PSALM 103:12 NKJV

Clean Slate

Guilt has two guises. It can be a fact or a feeling. A young man working part-time at a grocery store is guilty in fact if he takes snacks off the shelf to eat during his breaks. He may not *feel* guilty about it; perhaps he's new on the job, notices other employees doing it, and despite the tug of his conscience figures the store owner won't mind. However, the fact remains that he's stealing, breaking the law.

What if the young man sees his coworkers get caught, lose their jobs, and face prosecution for employee theft? Now, in addition to being guilty, he may feel shame and remorse. He may have a hard time looking the store owner in the eye. When the disciple Peter denied twice that he ever knew Jesus, he committed two grave offenses. Yet it wasn't until the third time, when Jesus caught his eye, that Peter realized the magnitude of what he'd done and wept bitterly.

Jesus completely forgave Peter. The great thing about God's promise to remove your guilt just as thoroughly is that it applies to both fact and feeling. God will deal with the root of any guilty emotions you may be carrying around, if you admit to him that you did wrong. Whatever your offense, God will eliminate it from the record entirely, restoring your sense of innocence. He will also help you face the consequences of your actions and make amends, so your earthly slate will be clean too.

> **Whatever your offense, God will eliminate it from the record entirely, restoring your sense of innocence.**

When God wipes a man's slate clean, it is clean indeed. Are you burdened with guilt? Ask God to forgive you and help you set things right, and then trust him to completely forget whatever wrong you committed.

The Spirit produces the fruit of love, joy, peace, patience, kindness, goodness, faithfulness, gentleness, self-control.

GALATIANS 5:22–23 NCV

Help with the Reins

A man's spirit is like a stallion that always wants to run wild. You need a lot of will power to bridle your spirit and make it obedient to God. Of course, if running wild produced a life of joy and contentment, there'd be no incentive for you to even try to restrain your urges and desires. But it's been said that discipline is freedom. The only way to experience true liberty and happiness is to gain control over the mustang inside you, and bring yourself into compliance with God's way of living.

How can you master such a willful beast? In the study of literature, conflict is classified into categories such as man against nature or man against man. In this case it's man against himself. Sometimes the hardest thing in the world to do is fight your own impulses. They can be so strong that it seems unnatural to deny them. It feels wrong to do the right thing. The key to winning this battle is to become so familiar with God's ways that you can recognize the difference between right and wrong despite your feelings.

> The only way to experience true liberty and happiness is to gain control over the mustang inside you.

Study the Bible thoroughly, and listen for God's voice whenever you're struggling with self-control. He will tell you clearly what you need to do, and then if you ask him, he will step into the fray and help you do it. Self-control is a misnomer, really; it's impossible to do it alone. Let God give you a hand with the reins.

—◎◎—

Ask God each day for the gift of self-control. It's a good gift, and it brings with it many other good gifts such as love and peace and goodness and joy.

By humility and the fear of the LORD are riches and honor and life.

PROVERBS 22:4 NKJV

The righteous man walks in his integrity; his children are blessed after him.

PROVERBS 20:7 NKJV

A Rich Legacy

When a man holds his child for the first time, he feels a powerful desire to be a good father. He begins to think about the kind of legacy he will pass on to his child. He knows that if he can be a good father, he'll leave behind not merely an investment portfolio but an inheritance that will enrich his child's life emotionally and spiritually, and similarly touch the lives of generations to follow.

According to the book of Proverbs, the key to being a good father is to be a good man. Your children will have a rich heritage if your life is above reproach. That's a tall order, but you can live faultlessly by maintaining an intimate relationship with your own heavenly Father. Through the Bible and his Spirit, God will teach you how to live a blameless life, and empower you to do it. If you cooperate with him, your children will profit enormously.

Living blamelessly means making a one-time, wholehearted commitment to obey God, then continually choosing to obey him for the rest of your life. It also involves always admitting to God any disobedi-

> **The key to being a good father is to be a good man.**

ence and getting right back in step with him. God will take away your guilt the moment you do, for he holds nothing against a man trying his best to obey him and asking for forgiveness whenever he fails. Such a man is deemed good, and his children will receive a tremendous inheritance— including an invaluable role model for their lives.

Do you really want to be a good father? Focus on being a good man. Commit yourself to living God's way, seek forgiveness for your mistakes, and he will reward both you and your children.

Six days a week are set apart for your daily duties and regular work, but the seventh day is a day of rest dedicated to the Lᴏʀᴅ your God.

Exᴏᴅᴜs 20:9–10 ɴʟᴛ

Weekly Respite

With the time pressures men face, trying to obey God's command to designate every Sunday as a special day can be a real challenge. But God has tangible rewards for the man who can take the calendar by the horns, wrestle it to the ground, and brand Sunday as unique. Before saddling up, however, there are two core truths about Sunday that you must know. They're important to recognize because men struggle in different ways when it comes to realizing the benefits of this day—some miss out because of work, some because of play.

First, God chose Sunday as a day for you to relax and recuperate. It's ironic that you have to fight hard just to take it easy. But often you *must* fight for what's important, and taking time to revitalize yourself is essential. If you habitually work seven days a week, your battle will be to cut your workweek down to six. You may have to adjust your lifestyle, but it'll be worth it.

> **Make Sunday a day to focus on God in prayer and worship. You'll find refreshment for your body, mind, and spirit.**

Second, God chose Sunday as a day for you to honor him. It's not just a day of rest. This truth may be just as challenging for you as the first one is for other men, if you normally spend all your Sundays watching sports or pursuing hobbies. Work hard to establish a good balance between recreation and dedication—that is, make Sunday a day to focus on God in prayer and worship. You'll find refreshment for your body, mind, and spirit.

You'll always find time for whatever is most important to you. Honor God on Sundays by showing him that he means more to you than either work or play.

Strength! Courage! Don't be timid; don't get discouraged. GOD, your God, is with you every step you take.

JOSHUA 1:9 MSG

No Fear

A man's life demands many levels of courage. It takes courage to work on a marriage, courage to stand up for your convictions, courage to start a new business, courage to be a father, courage to charge into battle, courage to fight a serious disease, courage to endure grief, courage to reach out to strangers, courage to admit mistakes. Some define courage as the ability to do what needs to be done in spite of fear. But the Bible offers something much better: the elimination of fear.

Joshua 1:9 unveils the foundation for courage. It's one of the great promises of God—that he will always be with you. To fully appreciate the impact of this promise, you have to understand who God is, what he is like. God is the Creator and sustainer of the universe. He is infinitely powerful, infinitely wise, and infinitely loving. He is eternal and

> **Nothing is impossible for God.**

never changes. He knows all about the past, present, and future, and he is ultimately in control of everything. The Bible describes him as a mighty rock, an impenetrable shield, an invincible stronghold, an unconquerable fortress. Nothing is impossible for God. It's no wonder Jesus told his followers not to be afraid.

This is one promise worth meditating on and remembering. If you understand its implications, put your trust in it, and bring it to mind whenever life calls you to be courageous, you'll be a different man, one who's never afraid to do what's right.

It's easy to be brave when you know God and know he is with you. Memorize Bible verses that describe him and remind you of his presence, and recall them when you need courage.

The LORD shall preserve you from all evil;
He shall preserve your soul.

PSALM 121:7 NKJV

Ultimate Security

Where should a man's sense of security be invested? In the government and the police? In a home-security system? In a gun next to his bed? During biblical times, the people of Israel were constantly placing their confidence in kings, armies, protective walls, and weapons. Again and again God showed them that he was their true source of security.

When God told an Israelite named Gideon to defend his people against the hordes of enemies encamped in their lands, Gideon raised up an army of more than thirty thousand men. But God whittled Gideon's forces down to just three hundred, so the Israelites would know that it was God who had saved them. In another instance, God acted alone, simply wiping out a huge enemy army overnight. At such times there was no doubt who Israel's protector was.

Men should take steps to ensure the safety of their nation, their communities, and their homes. However, God declares that unless he is in the picture, those trying to provide security are wasting their time. Only God can guarantee protection. As the preeminent guard in your life, God will help you look after your wife, your children, and your property. God, who never sleeps, will be vigilant twenty-four hours a day. He will provide you and your loved ones with ultimate security: freedom from worry and fear in this lifetime, and a carefree existence with him ever after.

> **Only God can guarantee protection.**

Invest your sense of security in God. Pray daily, thanking him for his protection and asking him to continue watching over you and yours. You'll breathe a lot easier, and sleep much better.

Whoever desires to become great among you, let him be your servant. And whoever desires to be first among you, let him be your slave—just as the Son of Man did not come to be served, but to serve.

MATTHEW 20:26–28 NKJV

The Mark of Greatness

What if the sports world celebrated greatness according to Jesus's definition? The most valuable baseball cards would feature bat boys. Football fans would give standing ovations to the guy in charge of the Gatorade cooler. Tennis lovers would seek autographs from the people who retrieve balls for the officials. And basketball's hall of fame would honor the fellows who run out every time a player falls down and wipe sweat off the court.

Few men aspire to such menial jobs. Businesses find it difficult to fill low-paying, unglamorous service positions, even during times of rising unemployment. Most men want to achieve a higher level of success. But when Jesus's followers started jockeying for rank under his leadership, he put a stop to it, declaring that the humble act of meeting others' needs is the truest mark of greatness. He offered himself as the prime example, labeling himself a servant and telling them that if they really wanted to be somebody, they should follow his career path.

> **When Jesus's followers started jockeying for rank under his leadership, he put a stop to it, declaring that the humble act of meeting others' needs is the truest mark of greatness.**

You can be a caregiver like Jesus no matter what your status in life. What makes a man a servant is his modest, selfless attitude about his own needs, and his loving and willing attitude toward helping others. Jesus said that by looking after people the way he did, a man will rise to prominence.

~⋙

Find practical ways to assist the people around you. Each day presents countless opportunities for you to walk in the footsteps of the greatest man who ever lived. Be on the lookout for them.

We also have joy with our troubles, because we know that these troubles produce patience. And patience produces character, and character produces hope.

ROMANS 5:3–4 NCV

End Product

A debilitating injury can strike a man hard, causing him to suffer not only physically but also emotionally, by attacking his sense of self-worth. However, God can use such times of pain so that rather than breaking you, they make you stronger, and instead of causing you to despair, they create in you a rock-solid optimism. One of the most wonderful traits of God is his ability to take the black coal of suffering and transform it into the shining diamond of hope.

If you turn to God for help when you're hurting, he does much more than comfort you. He gives you the fortitude you need to bear pain courageously. This inner strength changes your very nature. Surviving a difficult time makes you a better man, one equipped for the additional trials life is sure to bring along. That in itself gives you confidence for the days ahead.

> One of the most wonderful traits of God is his ability to take the black coal of suffering and transform it into the shining diamond of hope.

Even more important, by sustaining you through a time of pain, God will prove to you that your trust in him is well placed. The end product of suffering with God at your side is a greater hope in him, gained through both seeing how he can strengthen you and experiencing his faithfulness. Best of all, your increased assurance in God applies not just to this life but also to the next, leaving you with joyful anticipation for the future he has promised, a time in which there will be no more suffering.

Invite God into your difficult times and allow him to mold you in the midst of them. Turn this key that releases his power to ultimately bring hope out of pain.

W hat we see will last only a short time,
but what we cannot see will last forever.

2 CORINTHIANS 4:18 NCV

Optical Illusion

How close does this come to describing your idea of a perfect life: a beautiful wife, beautiful children, a beautiful home on beautiful property, a great-looking car, a cool boat or motorcycle, and smiling back at you in the mirror every morning, a handsome specimen of manhood in attractive clothes? You might dismiss all this as shallow, but it reflects a deep yearning in the heart of every guy. The desire for beauty is a powerful force in a man's life.

You could spend all your days chasing the beauty you see around you, and trying to improve your own appearance. But the world's beauty is fleeting and never really satisfies. The truth is, physical beauty is an illusion. What you really want—what you really need—is genuine beauty, which lasts forever and proves itself true because it emanates from a source of pure goodness and love.

Let your profound desire for beauty drive you to God. His beauty is authentic—and could never be described as skin-deep. It's an incomparable loveliness that's completely intertwined with his character. If you have faith, one day you'll see God face-to-face, and you'll be amazed. In the meantime, ask God to

> **Physical beauty is an illusion. What you really want—what you really need—is genuine beauty, which lasts forever.**

help you see and appreciate eternal beauty in this life. It's a reflection of his splendor, and it's all around. Real, unfading beauty shines from each man and woman in whom God is forming that person's character into the likeness of his own.

Determine to spend the rest of your life focusing on the things that have eternal beauty and value, the things that matter most to God. Study the Bible so you'll begin to recognize those things.

The heavens tell of the glory of God. The skies display his marvelous craftsmanship. Day after day they continue to speak; night after night they make him known.

PSALM 19:1–2 NLT

A Masterpiece of Design

Most guys love to be outside. They can't wait to get out of the house or office and immerse themselves in nature. Whether it's walking through the woods on an autumn morning, kayaking across a lake on a summer day, skiing in the mountains on a winter afternoon, or playing golf at sunset in the spring, men find joy and peace amid God's creation. Spending time outdoors refreshes their souls.

The poetic language and expansive imagery in this psalm evoke the grandeur of both creation and Creator. Reading them is like stepping outside and taking a breath of fresh air. Contemplating them is like gazing at the stars and seeing the fingerprints of God. Why do men leave the buildings they've constructed and venture out into the environment God so wonderfully designed? Because whether men realize it or not, creation speaks to men of a power and a wisdom and a glory that far exceed their own.

> Creation speaks to men of a power and a wisdom and a glory that far exceed their own.

Deep in his being, a man knows he could never create something as marvelous as a tree. He can chop one down, cut it into lumber, and build a house, but it's beyond him to produce a living organism that gathers energy from soil and sunlight, grows tall, attains a singular beauty, provides shelter, food, and oxygen for other living things, and miraculously reproduces itself. A masterpiece always attests to the reality of a master, and the incredible design of nature bears eloquent witness to the existence of God.

~~~

Anytime you can get outdoors to enjoy the free exhibition of God's spectacular artistry, take advantage of the opportunity to talk to the Artist. Allow the wonders of nature to lead you nearer to God.

Examine yourselves as to whether you are in the faith. Test yourselves.

2 CORINTHIANS 13:5 NKJV

Checking the Mirror

A man must never be afraid to ask himself whether he really is living God's way. It's a vital matter, and you need to know for sure one way or the other. Like a businessman monitoring his company for quality control, put yourself to the test regularly. If you discover that your life is on track, you'll be reassured; if you find it isn't, you can take steps to set it right.

It's possible to start out well with God and then falter, like a young plant that's growing strong but begins to be choked off by weeds. Sometimes life's concerns or the lure of wealth can cause a man to start concentrating on the wrong things and eventually lose sight of God. This can happen imperceptibly over a long period of time, so it's beneficial to take a hard look at your life now and then to determine where your focus is.

> It's beneficial to take a hard look at your life now and then to determine where your focus is.

Test your life for evidence that you're following Jesus. Is your character becoming more like his? Are your actions in line with behavior that pleases God? Sometimes a retrospective view makes it easier to spot telltale signs. How are you different now than you were a year or two ago? Seek input from people you trust. Can they see how God has been changing you? Finally, evaluate your connection with God. Are you still sensitive to his voice? Checking yourself in the mirror like this will help you keep your sights directly on him.

Maintain the caliber of your relationship with God at the highest level by examining yourself periodically. Enlist God's help, asking him to reveal your weak areas and affirm your areas of strength.

Resist the devil and he will flee from you.

JAMES 4:7 NKJV

The Devil

The devil bombards every man with thoughts of wrongdoing, such as blaming a coworker for his own mistake. It's war, so start thinking like a warrior. Get to know your enemy. Success on any battlefield depends on being aware of the opposition's strength, abilities, and tactics. If your knowledge about the devil is rudimentary, recognize that the Bible is your best source of intelligence about his characteristics, his intentions, and his MO. The more you understand your foe, the better. The most important thing to remember is that if you defy him, he'll retreat.

The Bible is also your most effective weapon against the devil. Jesus proved this when the devil accosted him in the desert. Every time the devil tried to make Jesus disobey God, Jesus shot him down by citing truths from the Bible. Knowing these truths enabled Jesus to refute the devil's lies. The devil can't fight truth; he had no choice but to give up and leave.

> **Recognize that the devil is your enemy. The biggest lie of all is that he's your friend.**

The key to victory against the devil is your response to him. The Bible is a powerful sword when it's drawn, and God will help you overcome your enemy. But you must recognize that the devil is your enemy. The biggest lie of all is that he's your friend. Ask God to show you if you're cooperating with the devil in any way. Oppose this foe wherever you encounter him. The devil will turn tail and run, as he's known to do.

Learn to perceive the devil's lies, reject them, and hold your ground against him. Always remember that you have allies in the battle to do what's right—both God and the truth.

The prayer of a person living right with God is something powerful to be reckoned with.

JAMES 5:16 MSG

The Vital Link

If you're like most men, you want your life to matter, to make a difference in the lives of others. That's a potent incentive to live God's way, according to James. On the human level, your influence in this world is limited to where you can go and what you can do and say. But on the spiritual level, you can have an unlimited impact on the world through your prayers, if you live according to God's plan.

Long ago God decided that Jesus, who always did what was right, would act as a middleman between himself and others. That's a great gift to anyone who is less than perfect.

However, having Jesus as an intermediary doesn't let you off the hook in terms of improving your behavior. If you want your prayers to be heard, you must maintain a relationship with him that keeps you moving ever closer to the pure lifestyle that pleases God.

Jesus promised his followers that God would grant them anything they asked for in his name, so many men include the phrase "in Jesus's name" in their prayers. If you do, reflect on what this phrase means to you. Is it simply a way to wrap up your prayers when you're finished?

> **You can have an unlimited impact on the world through your prayers, if you live according to God's plan.**

Are you using it as a magical phrase to ensure that your wishes come true? Determine never to use these words lightly, but to back them up with a wholesome lifestyle that demonstrates your connection to Jesus. That's what vitalizes prayer.

Are you living right with God through a relationship with Jesus? If so, pray confidently and expectantly, as a favored son making a request of a Father who is very pleased with him.

Love satisfies all of God's requirements.

ROMANS 13:10 NLT

Main Assignment

You have to meet certain conditions to pass a college course. There are homework assignments, projects, tests, and a final exam. But sometimes you can receive credit for a class by testing out of it, proving you've mastered the material. Knowledge will fulfill all the course requirements. Love has the same effect on God's stipulations. If a man could demonstrate perfect proficiency at loving God and loving others, he'd be in compliance with every command God made.

Only Jesus has ever accomplished that. Small wonder, when you read the Bible and learn what God means when he talks about love. It begins with concepts very challenging to put into practice, and goes on from there. For a man today, love starts with being patient with other drivers, being kind to telemarketers, being happy for friends who earn more than you, and being humble around those who earn less. It means being polite to the waiter who serves you, being more thoughtful of the needs of the person holding up the line than of your own, and being slow to take offense from anyone but quick to let it go.

> **If a man could demonstrate perfect proficiency at loving God and loving others, he'd be in compliance with every command God made.**

Love that satisfies God reflects his own, and here it gets tough. The best picture of God's love in the Bible is Jesus on the cross, forfeiting himself for the welfare of others. This sacrificial kind of love, in which a man gives his life away—in a moment or over a lifetime—is at the core of all God's commands.

Through pure love, Jesus has fulfilled all of God's requirements on your behalf. Ask God to develop in your heart a love just as perfect as his.

God so loved the world that He gave His only begotten Son, that whoever believes in Him should not perish but have everlasting life.

JOHN 3:16 NKJV

Open Invitation

If you've always wondered what the deal was with the guy in the end zone holding the sign that reads, "John 3:16," now you know. It's a declaration of how much God cherishes you. It's an attestation of how much he was willing to do for you. And it's an invitation for you to have a relationship with him that will never end.

Perhaps you were aware of what "John 3:16" means, but you've resisted the invitation because it seems strange that all you have to do to live forever with God is put your trust in Jesus. Yet that's the way God intends it. A guy in the Old Testament named Naaman almost missed his chance to be healed of leprosy because he couldn't believe that all God required of him was to bathe in the Jordan River. He was a happy man when God's prescription worked.

> **God loves the world—that's everybody.**

Today men around the world show their faith in God's mysterious ways by being baptized as followers of Jesus, knowing that trusting God brings eternal joy.

You may think God's invitation sounds exclusive. But read it again. God loves the world—that's everybody. His promise is for whoever believes that Jesus was his Son and died to save humankind—that's anybody. God's invitation is open to every man. His love for the world is enough to inspire a guy to make a fool of himself before millions of football fans to get the message across. That guy knows it's an invitation worth accepting.

〰

Always do things God's way, no matter how odd his methods seem. There's sure to be rich reward. In the case of God's incredible invitation, accepting his unusual terms results in eternal life.

The prayer of faith will save the sick, and the Lord will raise him up.

JAMES 5:15 NKJV

Primary Physician

Faith is not some vague, nebulous thing; it's simply an investment of trust. When a man pays health insurance premiums, or allows them to be deducted from his paycheck, he's putting his trust in the insurance company, counting on it to pay for medical care. Likewise, when he goes to the hospital, he's placing his confidence in the skill of doctors and the effectiveness of medicine, relying on them to cure him.

Your faith—in terms of healing—may begin here. It may end here too, or perhaps in addition to your trust in the healthcare system, you have some hope that God will also help heal you. God invites you to make him your primary physician. He encourages you to invest your highest trust in him, not abandoning the healthcare system but going to him first and asking him to make you well.

> **God has an advantage over every other healthcare provider: only he can heal a man forever.**

Prayer that expresses this kind of faith is the most essential part of the healing process, and should precede everything else.

When you are sick or injured, put your trust in God. He may restore you directly—he certainly has the power to do so. Or he may guide you to the right doctor and the best treatment and use them to heal you. God will always respond to your prayers; Jesus said that even if a man who believes in him dies, he will still live. God has an advantage over every other healthcare provider: only he can heal a man forever.

Select God as your primary physician. Trust him for healing whenever you or your loved ones are sick or injured, and ask him to guide you in determining what to do about medical treatment.

When you do a charitable deed, do not let your left hand know what your right hand is doing, that your charitable deed may be in secret; and your Father who sees in secret will Himself reward you openly.

MATTHEW 6:3–4 NKJV

Hidden Offerings

Sometimes the best way for a man to express his devotion to God is not by singing praise songs in a church full of people. Instead, it's by making a covert sacrifice on behalf of someone else, for no other reason than because he loves God and cares about the needy. The world may be unaware of his donation to a homeless shelter, for example, but God will never forget his kindness and generosity, and he will honor him for it.

When you make such a clandestine offering, you should do it so stealthily that you even hide it from yourself. How do you accomplish that? Well, it's kind of a left-brain, right-brain thing. On the one hand, you have a clear grasp intellectually on your budget and how much you've decided to set aside for charitable giving each month. On the other hand, you're so full of gratitude for all God has done for you that when you see a person in need, you're moved to respond, knowing that later the accountant in you will be cutting back your discretionary spending for a few weeks.

> A man's hidden gift is nothing that needs to be announced publicly; it's simply something he wants to give.

A man's hidden gift is nothing that needs to be announced publicly; it's simply something he wants to give. It's his own private act of worship toward God, a secret meant to be kept between the two of them. The man offering such a gift senses that God is pleased with him, and it's the only recognition and thanks he needs.

⁓⫯⧉

The next time you do a good deed, do it anonymously. God sees your charitable acts—trust him to repay you for all of them. The simple joy of giving is part of his reward.

He who sows bountifully will also reap bountifully.

2 CORINTHIANS 9:6 NKJV

God's Economy

Financial planners advise setting up a budget and establishing short- and long-term goals. They recommend putting money to work for you by selecting investments that provide an acceptable balance of risk and return. They counsel you to make sure your portfolio is diversified, and to carry adequate health, disability, and life insurance. They suggest that you seek out strategies to minimize your taxes each year, and engage in careful estate planning. Sounds like good advice. But following the recommendations of a financial expert may be insufficient to ensure that a man is managing his money wisely.

To be truly wise with your money, consult God on the subject. You may be surprised to learn that the Bible has a lot to say about finances. And the greatest principle in God's economy is this: Before all else, give a generous portion of your income to him. The more you are willing to give, the more handsomely he will reward you.

> **To be truly wise with your money, consult God on the subject.**

God's rewards will be more than financial. Money given to God and his work will be returned to you from unexpected and often unanticipated directions. He will repay your "sowing" in many ways. The apples you pick off the tree are different from the seed you plant in the ground. Yet the fruit does contain seeds; God will provide for your financial needs. Most important, he will put the money you give him to its best possible use, improving the lives and destinies of people in need.

Make it your habit to give generously to God. He will reward you in countless ways, not the least of which is the great feeling of knowing that you're making a difference in the world.

My true disciples produce much fruit.
This brings great glory to my Father.

JOHN 15:8 NLT

Measure of Productivity

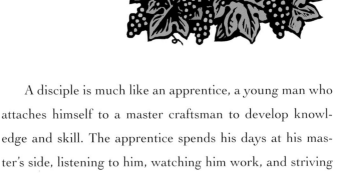

A disciple is much like an apprentice, a young man who attaches himself to a master craftsman to develop knowledge and skill. The apprentice spends his days at his master's side, listening to him, watching him work, and striving to emulate him. The outcome of this unique bond is twofold: over time, the apprentice becomes more and more like his master, and his handiwork begins to take on the same quality.

The greatest Master of all, Jesus, offers all men a wonderful promise. He doesn't say you *must* generate excellent results in order to join him, but rather guarantees that by affixing yourself to him as his apprentice, you *will*. He himself empowers you to grow and achieve. Being connected to God enables you to perform in the same way that plugging a personal computer into an electrical outlet brings it to life and allows it to be used to accomplish incredible things.

Using a different analogy, one that men from any time period would understand, Jesus described himself as a grapevine and his followers as branches. Just as a branch of a grapevine must be attached to the main vine to bear fruit, you must have an intimate relationship with Jesus to

> **Being connected to God enables you to perform in the same way that plugging a personal computer into an electrical outlet brings it to life.**

show results that please God. It's Jesus's life flowing through you that allows you to produce growth in your character and an impact on others' lives. That's the outcome God seeks.

Connect with God, and stay connected, by inviting him to be your Master and recommitting yourself to him each day. He desires that attachment with you but always gives you the freedom to choose.

Use honest scales and weights and measures.

LEVITICUS 19:36 MSG

Doing Business Right

In ancient times, when men making business transactions weighed silver or gold on a scale to determine its worth, unscrupulous dealers would often use inaccurate counterweights to get the better end of the bargain. Times haven't changed much since then, as evidenced by the rise of corporate fraud and identify theft. There are countless ways to cheat today, and some men put an incredible amount of thought and effort into devising schemes to take advantage of others.

Throughout history, God has always been delighted with men who operate aboveboard. Putting some thought and effort into ensuring that you act fairly in every area of your life, professional and personal, will please God greatly.

God approves of a man who is up-front with clients, fills out expense reports with integrity, is truthful when filing his income taxes, and tells the cashier when she hands him too much

> **God has always been delighted with men who operate aboveboard.**

change. You have many opportunities each day to be honest, and each one is your chance to bring God joy and gain his favor by choosing to do things his way.

Shooting straight in all your financial affairs is an essential aspect of being a godly, honorable man. Just as surely as God will repay you for giving part of your income to him, he will reward you for committing yourself to a standard of complete honesty in all your dealings with others. You have much to gain from doing business right.

Do everything with honesty, proving yourself faithful in the smallest of matters. Then God will know you'll be upright in the important matters, and he will entrust you with more and more.

I have set before you life and death,
blessing and cursing; therefore choose life.

DEUTERONOMY 30:19 NKJV

Yours for the Choosing

Business managers are constantly making important decisions. Part of what makes their job difficult is that they always operate with limited information. Often they must make crucial choices without the benefit of pertinent facts. The best managers gather as much data as possible, read between the lines as necessary, and use both judgment and intuition in deciding upon a course of action.

In many ways the need to make educated guesses carries over into a man's personal affairs. But that's not the case with life's most important choice. God provides you with all the facts you need to make this life-or-death decision. Read the Bible, take a look at the world with open eyes, pray for understanding, and you'll know everything you need to know. Once you've assessed the situation, evaluated the alternatives, and considered all the ramifications of your choice, it's an easy decision to make. God knows everything, and he has already shared his heartfelt recommendation.

> God doesn't pull any punches; he just lays it on the line.

God doesn't pull any punches; he just lays it on the line: "Here's your choice. Here's what I would do, but it's up to you." A life full of peace and joy and fulfillment is yours if you want it. You don't have to earn it; all you have to do is choose it. This involves surrender, a willingness to obey God and live life his way. But if you elect that option, you'll find it's the best choice you could possibly make.

God is offering you a choice that's both infinitely important and surprisingly simple. Don't make it more complicated than it is, and don't wait too long to make it. You don't want to miss this opportunity.

Pursue righteousness, godliness, faith, love, patience, gentleness. Fight the good fight of faith.

1 TIMOTHY 6:11–12 NKJV

Tender Warriors

Gentlemen have a call to be gentle as well as to be men. God has designed you to be strong, but he has also given you the capacity to be tender. In the movie *Camelot*, King Arthur instituted a new way of life in the Middle Ages by harnessing the energy of a privileged class of knights, whose horses, armor, and weapons allowed them to lord it over the common people. He exhorted them to valiantly use their might for the good of others. In a similar way, God calls the knights of his round table to be chivalrous. He expects them to be gentle men, tender warriors.

A gentle man doesn't snap at someone who interrupts him on the job; instead he takes time to listen to the person and offer help. A tender warrior doesn't allow an injustice to others to slip past him, but rather challenges it boldly. Gentle men consider the needs and feelings of the people in their lives. Tender warriors hold fast to their convictions when faced with a moral dilemma.

> **Help God bring chivalry back into vogue.**

Help God bring chivalry back into vogue. It involves much more than opening doors for others—although that's a good beginning. Chivalry is a code of honor that incorporates respect, thoughtfulness, courtesy, stout-heartedness, heroism, and valor. It signifies an inner strength that allows you to protect and serve others while you contend for what's right.

Strive for the qualities that make up a gentle man. Each of them are available to you. They reflect God's qualities, and you acquire them through a relationship with him.

Jesus said to them, "Because of your unbelief; for assuredly, I say to you, if you have faith as a mustard seed, you will say to this mountain, 'Move from here to there,' and it will move; and nothing will be impossible for you."

MATTHEW 17:20 NKJV

Mountaineering

Sir Edmund Hillary is a national hero in New Zealand, and renowned worldwide, for being the first man to climb Mount Everest. Jesus taught his followers a different way to conquer mountains. If they could learn to put the tiniest amount of trust in the power of God, he said in effect, they wouldn't have to claw their way up a mountain; they could simply ask God to remove it from their path.

Of course, Jesus was speaking figuratively. His followers had been trying to help a man with a serious problem.

The problem had proved insurmountable for them, so the man went to Jesus, who was immediately able to solve it. Jesus's followers came to him privately and asked why they had failed, and that's when Jesus enlightened them about the secret of mountaineering.

> **A mountain may seem awfully big to you, but to God it's just a bump on the planet.**

To understand this secret, you have to envision three things in proper scale. First, God's power. The Bible says that *everything* is possible with God. Imagine how vast his ability is. Second, the problem at hand. A mountain may seem awfully big to you, but to God it's just a bump on the planet. Third, the amount of faith you need. Jesus compared that to a minuscule seed—and the amazing thing is, the faith of his most loyal followers, men who'd left everything for him, didn't measure up. That's sobering, but you have access to something they didn't yet: God's Spirit living inside you, ready to increase your faith if you ask.

Refuse to be intimidated by the size of any problem you're facing. Focus on the immensity of God's power to help you, and put your trust in him.

This is My beloved Son, in whom I am well pleased.

MATTHEW 3:17 NKJV

Attaboys

It's tough for a man to be a celebrity these days, because he must constantly reinvent himself to remain popular with fans, whose likes and dislikes are always changing. But that's one of the problems with being a people pleaser, and you'll have to deal with that and other issues if you primarily look to others—such as your father, your boss, your wife, or your peers—for recognition and support.

The best alternative is not to become your own man, trying to make it through life without the affirmation you need, but rather to become God's man—such as the employee who disobeys his boss's "suggestion" to cook the books a bit. This is a deeply significant transformation in which, by placing your trust in Jesus and identifying yourself with him, you are adopted as God's own son and begin living for his approval alone.

A son of God receives God's affirmation simply for being who he is. When Jesus was baptized, God's Spirit came down from heaven to settle on him, as if his Father were laying a hand on his shoulder. Then he heard God say how much he loved

> A son of God receives God's affirmation simply for being who he is.

him and how delighted he was with him. This was before Jesus had delivered one sermon or performed a single miracle. Later God reaffirmed Jesus on a mountaintop, during a time when Jesus's initial popularity with the people had waned. As God's son, you too will enjoy his unwavering dedication and support, a continuous reminder of your worth.

Start living for God's approval; it will free you from the need to follow the crowd. Pursue the path in life God has laid out for you, knowing you'll always have his love and encouragement.

Don't set your heart on anything that is your neighbor's.

EXODUS 20:17 MSG

Considering the Joneses

The scuba instructor seemed to be the most likable guy in the world when you signed up for lessons. But now as you sit dangling your feet in the water, he starts laying down the rules. Suddenly the ocean doesn't seem like just a big playground anymore. You chafe at the restrictions, but as he discusses the importance of using the buddy system, monitoring your air supply, keeping calm if your mask gets knocked off, and ascending slowly to avoid the bends, you realize he must care a lot about your well-being.

What does the bottom of the ocean a.k.a. Davy Jones's locker have to do with the Joneses' new motor home? When God issues rules—especially one of the Ten Commandments, like this one—he always has a man's best interest in mind. The Bible says envy will rot your bones. God knows that jealousy is extremely unhealthy for you, just as a

> **Trust God enough to heed his commands.**

scuba instructor knows that rising to the surface quickly will cause severe damage to your body.

Maybe you've always thought God would be much more likable if he weren't so bossy. But when you really consider things, aren't you glad he hasn't tossed you into life's ocean with no clue as to its opportunities or its perils? Trust God enough to heed his commands, and you'll evade threats such as envy. You'll find yourself truly free to enjoy life's wonders, and you'll discover that God is far more likable—even lovable—because he cares so deeply about you.

Purge envy out of your heart the way a diver clears water out of his mask, by displacing it. Ask God to fill your heart with joy and peace, so jealousy will be forced out.

H e leads me in the paths of
righteousness for His name's sake.

PSALM 23:3 NKJV

Asking for Directions

Most guys are comfortable with compasses and maps.
They are visually oriented and think in terms of north, east,
south, and west. Give them a map and a compass, and they
can readily find their way from point A to point B. Problems
arise when they're traveling with nothing but a map in their
head and their own sense of direction. They may be completely lost, but their confidence in their own navigational
abilities—and perhaps their pride—prevents them from
asking somebody for assistance.

God provides you with a great deal of guidance if you choose to live a life that will please him. The Bible is like a map with a "You are here" arrow, showing where you're at in relation to God. It also indicates the main roads that are acceptable to him, and those that are not. For example, the highway named Marital Faithfulness is highlighted yellow, while Infidelity is colored red. God's Spirit is like a compass giving you specific, personal instruction. For instance, his Spirit might direct you to take a side street called Marriage Counseling.

> God's Spirit is like a compass giving you specific, personal instruction.

Become more familiar with the Bible than you are with a map of your own country. Learn how to interpret the signals of God's Spirit better than you can read a compass. And don't hesitate to ask someone who knows which way is north to show you the way. You can depend on God to use all three to point you in the right direction.

God will always show you the best roads in life, but he will never force you to travel them. Every morning, make a commitment to seek and trust his guidance for the day.

The LORD shall preserve
you from all evil; He shall
preserve your soul.

PSALM 121:7 NKJV

As iron sharpens iron, so a man sharpens the countenance of his friend.

PROVERBS 27:17 NKJV

Going It Together

In business and sports, competition keeps individuals, corporations, and teams razor-sharp. When it comes to living right, however, it's accountability that keeps a man well honed. Meeting regularly with one or more men who know God, love him, and are dedicated to following his ways will prevent you from growing dull around the edges.

This image of iron sharpening iron is a great picture of accountability and a good reminder of its importance. Just as a blacksmith uses a hammer and an anvil to forge a mighty sword, God will use other men to build and shape your character. The result is that you become a powerful instrument in God's hand, a man with whom he can do great things in the world. However, for this to occur, you have to make yourself available to others, the way men in the early days of the church devoted themselves to meeting together, learning from the apostles, and helping one another put this knowledge into practice.

Accountability involves permitting trusted friends to hold you to your commitment to godly living. There are many elements to the process. It's about praying for one another, encour-

> **Accountability involves permitting trusted friends to hold you to your commitment to godly living.**

aging each other, grieving and celebrating together, learning from one another's victories and mistakes. It means admitting struggles and coming clean about wrongdoing. Accountability is about laying your life open like a chessboard before other players who can help you see where you are doing well and where you need to strengthen your offense and defense so you will prevail.

Make yourself available to God so he can forge you into a mighty instrument for his purposes. Ask God to help you join a group of men who will provide the accountability you need.

Not by might nor by power, but by My Spirit.

ZECHARIAH 4:6 NKJV

Magnum Force

The trick to cutting lumber is to let the saw do the work. When you have a sharp blade in your hand, you don't have to force it through the wood. You do your part by moving the saw smoothly back and forth, and the blade does its job. Life with God is similar. You both have a role to play: yours is to bring God's Spirit to bear on whatever task is at hand, and his is to get it done. Actually, a handsaw analogy doesn't do this core principle justice. It's more like using a power saw.

The best thing you can do every morning is to connect with God by reading the Bible, contemplating its meaning, and asking him for assistance throughout the day. If you find this difficult, then it's the first activity God can help you with. Make your first waking thought a request that he will give you the desire and ability to plug into him. You'll be amazed at how quickly God will clear your head and jump-start your heart, and how rich and empowering your time with him will be.

> **Develop the practice of teaming up with God's Spirit. There's no need to struggle through life on your own.**

Develop the practice of teaming up with God's Spirit. There's no need to struggle through life on your own. Whether you're trying to clean up your own act or striving to accomplish some good in the world, if you learn what your part is and concentrate on doing it, God will do his—and with awesome effectiveness get the job done.

God puts incredible power in the hands of a man who's bent on living for him. Team up with God, align your purposes with his, and allow him to release his power in you.

W hoever hears these sayings of Mine, and does them, I will liken him to a wise man who built his house on the rock.

MATTHEW 7:24 NKJV

Foundation Work

Say you're building your own home, and the basement walls are already poured. As you start to put up the frame, is there any reason why you wouldn't locate it squarely on the foundation? Of course not. It would be foolish to place the house near the foundation but not on it, or only partly on it. Even a novice builder would understand that in this phase of construction, close or halfway doesn't cut it. He'd erect the entire frame directly on the footing.

Through his teachings, Jesus has laid the only sure foundation for living. It's in place, available for every man to build upon. There are others available too, but his is the only one that's thoroughly sound and will never crumble when put to the test. Each man must decide for himself which foundation he wants to use. If you choose Jesus's words as the basis for your life, you can enjoy stability, peace, and prosperity—depending, naturally, on the construction techniques you employ.

> **Each man must decide for himself which foundation he wants to use.**

It's not enough to build your house near the foundation, that is, to listen to Jesus's teachings but not put them into practice. Building part of your home on the foundation, or adhering to only some of his precepts, won't work either. However, complete obedience to Jesus's instructions—to trust God, forgive your enemies, be true to your word, and care for others—will release in your life all the benefits of the foundation Jesus laid, and provide you a secure, happy home.

Examine your life as it stands today. Is it built squarely on the foundation Jesus laid? Ask Jesus to guide you as you continue building your life in the future.

He who has begun a good work in you will complete it until the day of Jesus Christ.

PHILIPPIANS 1:6 NKJV

Work in Progress

At one time or another, every man has felt underdressed for the occasion. A college student who was meeting his dad at a restaurant was stopped because he wasn't dressed properly. The maître informed him that a jacket was required, then turned to a rack, picked one out, and helped him put it on. Wearing the oversize jacket over his T-shirt, the young man was now deemed to be appropriately attired, and he was politely escorted to his father's table. That's an illustration of justification, which is what Jesus did for you when he died on the cross. He placed a royal mantle over your shoulders, making you acceptable in God's sight despite your flaws.

It's the job of God's Spirit to change you on the inside, making you pure and without fault, just like God. This is called sanctification. It's a lifelong process that begins when you invite God's Spirit into your heart, and continues until either you go to heaven or Jesus returns to earth.

Sanctification is God's way of molding your character. It's how he helps you mature spiritually so you develop into a godly man, worthy of the immaculate garment Jesus gave you.

> It's the job of God's Spirit to change you on the inside, making you pure and without fault, just like God.

Sanctification is guaranteed to be effective. God will never give up on you, even when you feel like giving up on yourself. He will continue to perfect you until the beauty of your inner being matches the splendor of the regal cloak you wear, and you're ready to meet him face-to-face.

Cooperate wholeheartedly with God's Spirit, trusting God's promise to sanctify you. He will make dramatic improvements in your character immediately, and spend the rest of your life polishing you to perfection.

Foolish people lose their tempers, but wise people control theirs.

Proverbs 29:11 NCV

Keeping Your Cool

A teenager working in a fast-food restaurant may look silly in his little paper hat, but the guy yelling at him for giving him the wrong amount of French fries looks much more foolish. In God's eyes, he's wearing a big dunce cap. No man wants to be a fool, and using your head will help you keep your cool. One of the many aspects of godly wisdom is knowing how to handle your temper.

You shouldn't repress anger, of course. Stuffing down angry feelings isn't healthy emotionally, physically, or spiritually. It doesn't work anyway; anger will always come out somehow, often in inappropriate ways such as passive-aggressive behavior or sudden unprovoked outbursts. And unresolved anger will inevitably lead to bitterness. Anger needs to be expressed, but a smart man communicates his feelings in a controlled, constructive way, more like a pressure relief valve than an exploding boiler.

> A smart man communicates his feelings in a controlled, constructive way, more like a pressure relief valve than an exploding boiler.

Managing your anger is like controlling your dog when you live in a city. Obviously, you don't allow a dog to run wild; he might hurt somebody. Just as obviously, you don't keep him cooped up in an apartment all the time. He might hurt you. Instead, you walk him on a leash, keep him in a fenced-in yard, allow him to run around in the park as long as he obeys your commands. You give him some freedom but always stay in charge. Self-control is an important key to dealing with anger.

~

Be a wise man by learning how to manage your temper. Self-control is one key to handling anger; two others you'll need on your keychain are love and forgiveness.

Your heavenly Father already knows all your needs, and he will give you all you need from day to day if you live for him and make the Kingdom of God your primary concern.

MATTHEW 6:32–33 NLT

Life's Essentials

Most likely, God has long been fulfilling his promise to supply all you require. Chances are, he has always provided you with the things essential to your survival. If he hadn't, you wouldn't be reading this book. You've probably always had a roof over your head, food to eat, clothes to wear. The challenge at this point is to recognize that God is the one who has been meeting your needs; the challenge going forward is to trust him to keep doing so.

Addressing these challenges is important for men because if you realize that God is supplying your fundamental needs, you'll give him the director's chair in your life—the best thing any man can do. God deserves this prominent position and is capable of filling it. Putting God there instead of your employer or yourself frees you to concentrate on something even more important than life's necessities: fulfilling the role God has for you to play in his grand production. That's where Jesus recommended that every man fix his focus, promising that if you do, God will look after all the rest.

> **God is and has always been your sole provider.**

God is and has always been your sole provider. You can count on him to keep meeting all your needs. If you pour all your energy into following God's lead, he will supply you with all the food, shelter, and clothing you require. Best of all, under his direction the story of your life won't merely be about survival; it'll reflect a much higher purpose.

Make a concerted effort to stop worrying about your needs. God is aware of them before you even ask him. Dedicate yourself to what really matters in life—playing the part God has assigned you.

Workouts in the gymnasium are useful, but a disciplined life in God is far more so, making you fit both today and forever.

1 Timothy 4:8 msg

Strengthening Your Heart

Some guys overdo the physical fitness thing, while some don't do it enough. The apostle Paul told Timothy that staying in shape is helpful and good. Health professionals today also appreciate the value of exercise. It raises a man's level of energy, improves his emotional state, and increases his ability to think. A balanced regimen—weight training, aerobic activity, stretching exercises—produces strength, stamina, and flexibility. Exercise helps ward off illness and injury, contributing to a long, productive life. It's definitely worthwhile.

Yet Paul went on to say that there's something even more important. Your heart may benefit greatly from regular activity, but it needs more to be truly healthy. If you want your heart to be good, you have to get on a program that conditions you for a lifetime with God.

It takes self-control to stick with an exercise routine, and training with God is no different. So make a focused, concentrated effort not only to

> **It takes self-control to stick with an exercise routine, and training with God is no different.**

stay in shape but also to learn what God requires of you and to practice doing it. Schedule your workouts if necessary, and while you do, schedule a regular time each day to read the Bible. Sometimes you'll have to force yourself to exercise when you don't want to, and at times you'll need to push yourself to read the Bible and do what it says. But the payoff for discipline is huge. It's what got Rocky in prime physical shape, and it will make you healthy in body and spirit.

Condition your body for a lifetime by exercising, eating right, and getting plenty of sleep. Condition your spirit for eternity by studying the Bible, connecting with God through prayer, and obeying him.

Understand what the will of the Lord is.

EPHESIANS 5:17 NKJV

Climb
Aboard

In the Christmas film *The Polar Express*, a boy stands in the snow in the middle of the night, staring at the strange train that has stopped in front of his house. The conductor looks at him and says, "Well, you coming?" When the boy asks where they're going, he replies, "Why, to the North Pole, of course!" God's intent may seem as mysterious to you, a grown man, as the conductor's seemed to the boy, but once you comprehend where he wants to take you, you'll be enticed to join him.

God's infinite mind is beyond any man's ability to perceive, yet because he wants you to know his desire, in many ways it's like an open book. The Bible lays out his objective very clearly, and stresses the importance of understanding it.

When you do, you'll realize that God's ambition for you is perfectly good and pleasant. If you want the best life has to offer, climb aboard. God's aim is to fill you with love and peace and joy and hope. His design is for your life to be healthy, prosperous, meaningful, and productive.

> **God intends to transform you into a man who is patient, kind, faithful, and self-disciplined.**

God's goal is also to change you into the man he means you to be—a good man, noble, wise, and true. He meets you where you are, but he can't take you with him if he leaves you there. So God intends to transform you into a man who is patient, kind, faithful, and self-disciplined. It's part of the exciting, rewarding journey he has planned.

Show God you're on board with him by accepting his will and cooperating with him to fulfill it. Learn everything you can about his itinerary, and choose to make it yours.

If we confess our sins, He is faithful and just to forgive us our sins and to cleanse us from all unrighteousness.

1 JOHN 1:9 NKJV

Calling a Spade a Spade

Sometimes the most manly thing you can do is to confront your faults and admit your weaknesses, to take a hard look at your wrong conduct and call it exactly what it is. This takes humility, but it also requires maturity and courage. There's power in a name. Correctly identifying a problem in your life gives you the clarity you need to deal with it. Naming wrong behavior accurately cuts through any denial you may be hiding behind and forces you to face it head-on, like a real man.

How do you think God will react when you finally drop all your excuses and defenses and simply agree with the way he classifies your actions? That's all confession is, when it comes down to it. It's reading in the Bible that a spade is a spade, hearing God's Spirit whisper to you that a spade is a spade, and looking at the card in your hand—the behavior you know in your heart is wrong—and saying, "That's a spade."

> **Correctly identifying a problem in your life gives you the clarity you need to deal with it.**

Repentance is more than just confession, however. Repentance is deciding once and for all to lay down the card. God will rejoice when you do. He will honor your courage and humility, and he will reaffirm that you're not only a man but *his* man. Then, true to his merciful nature and his written promise, he will take the card and tear it up. It will never be held against you. It will never even be remembered.

Bravely confess your wrong behavior to God and to people you trust—your pastor, your wife, the men in your accountability group. Deal with wrongdoing squarely and courageously, and be free of it forever.

He who walks with integrity walks securely.

PROVERBS 10:9 NKJV

Solid Footing

Guys venture out on frozen lakes every winter to fish, snowmobile, and cross-country ski. Unfortunately, every now and then they fall through the ice, sometimes taking with them their equipment, their snowmobiles, even their pickup trucks. Suddenly a time of recreation and fun becomes a dangerous, life-threatening situation. The good news is, such accidents can be avoided if men will devote some time and effort to ensuring that the ice beneath them is safe.

There is wisdom in monitoring your footing to make certain it's firm. As you consider your character—your level of integrity, which serves as a foundation—do you have any reason to suspect you could be walking on thin ice? You may be feeling pretty good about yourself, but perhaps once in a while you notice a cracking sound, or feel something shifting beneath your feet. Now is a good time to examine your character, to drill down and find out how deep it goes.

> There is wisdom in monitoring your footing to make certain it's firm.

If you're not sure how to do this, start with prayer. The Bible says God tests a man's heart, checking for integrity. If you ask him, he will reveal to you the results he sees. Also, the Bible is the perfect standard by which to measure your character. If you compare your qualities with those that God says make up a good man, you will quickly find out how securely you're walking. It's a humbling thing, but be encouraged—God can also help you change your heart.

Remember that your integrity is a foundation not only for you but also for the people you love. Monitor your character and keep it strong, to ensure their well-being as well as your own.

Where your treasure is, there your heart will be also.

MATTHEW 6:21 NKJV

Self-Storage

In the Sermon on the Mount, Jesus shared a profound truth: a man's heart—the core of his passion, the essence of his being—will always be found with whatever he values most. It's a fact that hasn't changed in two thousand years. Today the key to a man's heart may very well have the number of a self-storage unit stamped on it. Jesus also noted that *everything* a man owns here on earth is subject to damage and loss. Since any man who loves temporary objects is guaranteed to wind up brokenhearted, Jesus offered a better alternative.

If your heart is locked up in self-storage or some other unlikely place, you should relocate it to heaven, where it will never be crushed. How? Simply by choosing heaven as the spot where your most prized possessions will reside. The key to this great storage facility, Jesus revealed later, is stamped with a word: *generosity*.

If you want to stockpile treasure in heaven, the kind that won't ever depreciate in worth and can never be taken away, you'll have to share your treasures here on earth. Jesus went so far as to tell a young man that he should sell all he owned and give the money to the poor. Yet Jesus also taught that a relationship with God—the most valuable possession any man can have—is a treasure worth giving up everything else to obtain.

> **If you want to stockpile treasure in heaven, the kind that won't ever depreciate in worth and can never be taken away, you'll have to share your treasures here on earth.**

Things that last, such as real estate, are worth more than those things that don't, such as automobiles. Where do you want to invest your passion—in a few years here on earth or in an eternity in heaven?

"Honor your father and mother," which is the first commandment with promise: "that it may be well with you and you may live long on the earth."

EPHESIANS 6:2–3 NKJV

A Son's Duty

If you were taught the Ten Commandments as a boy, when you grew up you may have mentally checked off the fifth one, thinking, *One down, nine to go.* Sorry to burst your bubble, but being a faithful son is a lifelong obligation. On the bright side, it's a duty that brings lots of honor—to you, your parents, and God. And God's command to treat your mother and father with the utmost respect carries with it his pledge that in doing so, you'll enjoy a good, long life.

Maybe God made this command one of the Big Ten because he knew that guys could use a reminder about how important it is for their parents to feel loved and appreciated. So there he put it, smack-dab in the middle of the stone tablets Moses carried down from Mount Sinai. It's an expression of how highly God values the parent-son relationship, which mirrors his relationship with you.

> It's a son's noble duty to honor his parents as long as they live, and to honor their memory when they're gone.

There are countless ways to show your parents your loyalty, affection, and esteem. You can call, e-mail, and visit them regularly, for a start. Take them out to lunch or offer to help around their house. Show an interest in their interests, and invite them along on family outings. Ask them for advice. Put up with their faults, forgive them for past failures, praise them, thank them, and look after them. It's a son's noble duty to honor his parents as long as they live, and to honor their memory when they're gone.

Begin honoring your father and mother today—it's never to late to start. If your relationship with one or both of them isn't good, ask God to help you take the first steps toward reconciliation.

He who has begun a good
work in you will complete it
until the day of Jesus Christ.

PHILIPPIANS 1:6 NKJV

Without counsel, plans go awry, but in the multitude of counselors they are established.

PROVERBS 15:22 NKJV

Getting Input

Much of what you might call conventional wisdom comes straight from the Bible. Long before someone coined the saying "Two heads are better than one," King Solomon—who had received great understanding from God—wrote about the need to get input from others. That's partly why it's such a good idea to familiarize yourself with the Bible: you'll know the difference between conventional wisdom, which you can often afford to ignore, and God's advice, which you'll always want to heed.

You might see a chance right now to make a big improvement in your life. Maybe it involves changing careers, or quitting your job and starting your own business, or taking the business you already own in a new direction. However, even if the opportunity seems ripe, you don't want to make such a decision without a lot of forethought and planning, especially if you're married and have a family to support. And if you're getting serious about doing things God's way, you'll want to pick some other people's brains as you engage your own.

> **Information from experts will help you consider all the ramifications of your choice.**

Information from experts will help you consider all the ramifications of your choice. The guys in your accountability group can offer valuable insight, from their own life experience and from their knowledge of what makes you tick. Remember too that your wife's input is priceless—both her thoughts about the opportunity and her sense of whether it's worthwhile. More and more it seems that a woman's intuition is another kind of wisdom directly from God.

⤳∭◎

Make God your most important adviser. Allow your wife, other men, and experts to help you figure out what God is telling you to do, then ask him to confirm it in your heart.

Take the wood out of your own eye. Then you will see clearly to take the dust out of your friend's eye.

MATTHEW 7:5 NCV

A Delicate Procedure

If you've ever had a splinter in your eye, you know it's no laughing matter. Jesus used a little hyperbole to address an important issue. Imagine you neglected to wear goggles while running your power saw, and you are sitting in an eye surgeon's office, waiting to have a tiny, irritating splinter removed. In walks the doctor, and to your horror his right eye is swollen shut. It turns out he was doing some woodworking too, and pierced his eye with a sliver as thick as a toothpick. While he gropes around for an instrument, you're heading out the door, convinced he's in no shape to operate.

If nothing else, this scenario should convince you of the need for safety glasses. Hopefully, it will convey another lesson as well: Confronting a person about some wrong he's committing is a delicate procedure, and you must be clear of wrongdoing yourself to be qualified to perform it. If you aren't, the person will dismiss you as unworthy to either judge him or help him straighten out his life.

> **Confronting a person about some wrong he's committing is a delicate procedure.**

The great promise in this verse is that you *can* get that log out of your eye, and if you do, others will see you as a man of integrity and be more open to what you say. Remember, though, that having clear sight is only the first prerequisite for this delicate procedure; you also need a gentle touch. Helping another person turn away from wrongdoing requires compassion.

Even an eye surgeon needs someone else to remove a splinter from his own eye. Get God's help to deal with your faults—especially before confronting others about theirs.

No temptation has overtaken you except such as is common to man; but God is faithful, who will not allow you to be tempted beyond what you are able, but with the temptation will also make the way of escape, that you may be able to bear it.

1 Corinthians 10:13 nkjv

Noble Retreat

Sometimes the best way to beat the allure of wrong behavior is to find the nearest exit. The way out may literally be through a door, as when you're standing in the video store lingering over a movie you know you shouldn't rent. But at times you'll have to search a little harder to locate a means of escape, as when you're out of town on a business trip, looking at the list of cable channels in your hotel room.

At times like these, your "emergency exit" may look something like an unplugged TV and a good book.

When the devil is trying to persuade you to disobey God and you need to make a quick getaway, remember that Jesus once described himself as a kind of door. He is always available when you choose to flee from temptation. As with every door, he leads you from one place to another. Every time you escape from the devil by running to Jesus, he takes you into the presence of God.

> **The devil can't make you do anything.**

The devil can't make you do anything. God will not allow him to entice you any more strongly than he has any other man who's ever lived. So you don't have to fear the devil; he can't harass you more than you can stand. Just get away from him as quickly as possible. Turn to Jesus as soon as you realize you're being tempted, and with your head held high make a fast but noble retreat.

Don't let the devil convince you to fill your legitimate needs in illegitimate ways. Escape this deadly trap God's way, by running to Jesus for all your needs instead.

Walk circumspectly, not as fools but as wise, redeeming the time.

EPHESIANS 5:15–16 NKJV

Precious Time

Men love their hobbies. A lot of guys are into remote-controlled airplanes. They spend many enjoyable hours building their aircraft, then devote additional time to learning to fly them. There's a vicarious freedom in watching your plane soar high above, and a certain satisfaction in practicing a new maneuver until you get it right. Of course, if that power dive you're working on goes wrong, you get to spend many more happy hours repairing your airplane or building a new one.

Leisure-time activities seem to fall right in line with the expression *Carpe diem*. It means "Seize the day"—in other words, "Forget about life for a while and grab the pleasure of the moment." It sounds similar to the Bible's admonition to "make the most of every opportunity," but the two concepts are opposed. God can use your spare time in meaningful ways, more than you can imagine, if you offer some of it to him. He'll show you how to invest it in people he cares about — starting with your own family.

> **God can use your spare time in meaningful ways.**

When you're out by yourself flying your plane, nothing matters but the wind and the sky. Other hobbies offer a similar escape, and sometimes a man needs that. But it's important to remember that time is a valuable, limited commodity, and to ask yourself whether you're spending it judiciously. If you sense that you're seizing too many of the moments God is giving you, your commitment to start making the most of them will please him.

God knows you need some recreation occasionally, but he can refresh your spirit in surprising ways. Try using some of your "me time" for others. You'll be amazed at how invigorated you'll feel.

Those who wait on the LORD shall renew their strength; they shall mount up with wings like eagles, they shall run and not be weary, they shall walk and not faint.

ISAIAH 40:31 NKJV

Healthy Energy

Life is very demanding. Sometimes you have no choice but to work long hours to finish a college paper, business report, or construction project. When you're putting in the overtime, physically and mentally exhausted and wanting nothing more than to rest, how do you find the energy to keep going?

You might rely on coffee or soda or over-the-counter stimulants, but they tend to keep you awake when you finally go to bed, and you lose even more sleep. You could reach for junk food, looking for an emotional lift and a sugar high to get you through the ordeal. Too much of that stuff won't do your heart or your waistline any favors, though. You might even be tempted to take a quick peek at some provocative images in a magazine or on the Internet to perk yourself up, but you realize how damaging that would be to your relationship with God and others.

> **Anytime you're feeling burned out but must press on, day or night, look to God for a burst of new life.**

The prophet Isaiah revealed a powerful, surefire method to regain your gusto—one that's healthy for you in every way. Simply ask God to invigorate you. You need a second wind, and the Bible describes God's Spirit as a mighty wind. God can certainly provide the pickup you need, and he will give it to you if you just ask for it. He can quickly reenergize your entire being. Anytime you're feeling burned out but must press on, day or night, look to God for a burst of new life.

~

Whether the challenge before you is demanding physically, mentally, emotionally, or spiritually, ask God to give you the strength to meet it. Rely on his power to sustain you.

Having been set free from sin, and having become slaves of God, you have your fruit to holiness, and the end, everlasting life.

Romans 6:22 NKJV

True Liberty

The apostle Paul laid out a wonderful progression that shows how a man can move from the darkest bondage to the brightest freedom. When a man enslaved to his own desires cries out to Jesus for help, Jesus offers to rescue him from his plight—providing that he also allows Jesus to be his "Lord," his new Master. So the man is released from the emptiness of living to please himself and steps into the richness of living to please God. Immediately he feels a sense of liberty, finding life under his new Master to be much more meaningful and fulfilling.

In the second stage of this progression, the man's very nature begins to change. That's because God's Spirit moved into his heart when Jesus became his Savior and Lord. Now the most distinct quality of God, holiness—God's perfect goodness—is present inside the man's being. Increasingly it becomes part of him. The process is complicated by the efforts of his former master to regain control. But as the man keeps choosing to serve God instead, he becomes

> When a man enslaved to his own desires cries out to Jesus for help, Jesus offers to rescue him from his plight.

more and more like his new Master, and experiences a greater and greater feeling of freedom.

The marvelous result of the progression Paul spelled out is a blissful, never-ending life with God in heaven. There a man finds complete liberation—freedom from the lure of inappropriate desires, freedom from the consequences of wrongdoing, and freedom to enjoy all the rewards his new Master has for him.

Becoming God's slave is the truest form of freedom. Make God your Master and commit yourself to serving him. Set yourself on the path of ever-increasing joy and liberation.

Rest in the LORD, and wait patiently for Him.

PSALM 37:7 NKJV

In Good Time

Several men in the Bible who thought their lives were going well went through an unexpected "dry spell" before their careers really took off. Moses, who had been educated in a pharaoh's palace, spent forty years in the desert tending sheep before becoming a mighty emancipator. Joseph, the privileged son of Jacob, was unjustly imprisoned for years before becoming a powerful ruler. Paul, who was a respected Jewish religious leader when he met Jesus, spent a good deal of time in obscurity in Arabia before becoming a great evangelist.

Your life may seem at a standstill right now. Perhaps you're certain of what you want to accomplish, but circumstances are holding you back. You may be confused because you're convinced that your plans match God's purpose for you here on earth. Day after day you find yourself restless, champing at the bit. Your frustration may be over your career, an avocation you're passionate about,

> **It's vital to remember that God is orchestrating the events in your life.**

some volunteer work you're involved in, or even a relationship that appears to be going nowhere.

As you endure this ordeal, it's vital to remember that God is orchestrating the events in your life. He is using the time. At the right moment God will open the gate and release you to run the course he is laying out for you. The race is sure to be exciting and rewarding. In the meanwhile, there's a peace to be found in trusting his perfect timing.

Are you making the most of your time while you await God's go-ahead? Spend it wisely by getting to know both him and yourself better. You'll be well prepared for whatever lies ahead.

As the heavens are higher than the earth, so are My ways higher than your ways, and My thoughts than your thoughts.

ISAIAH 55:9 NKJV

A Step Above

Men are remarkable beings. Their intelligence, manual dexterity, and emotional capacity put them far above all the rest of God's creatures. Men think and operate at a level greatly superior to that of any of the animals that inhabit this earth. As noble and magnificent as a twelve-point buck appears, there's no comparison between its thoughts and the hopes, dreams, and plans of the man hiking through the surrounding woods.

Without diminishing at all his own greatness, however, every man must come to terms with the truth that God is even further above man than man is above the animals.

Infinitely more so. God's simplest thought reaches beyond the most profound contemplation of any man who ever lived. God's "1 + 1 = 2" is greater than Einstein's "$E = MC^2$." To the same extent, God's weakest display of strength far surpasses man's most powerful expression of might, to the point where what's impossible for a man is an easy matter for God.

> God's simplest thought reaches beyond the most profound contemplation of any man who ever lived.

This is good news. Far from making you feel inferior, grasping this truth will give you a deeper appreciation for how wonderfully you were created by such an awesome God. It will also give you a sense of confidence and security, knowing you can depend on God's wisdom instead of your own, and can rely on his strength rather than yours. If you belong to God through faith in Jesus, God's superior wisdom and exceeding power are available for you.

Anytime you have a chance to enjoy the wonders of nature, remind yourself that you are the crown of God's creation—and that this God who is greater than you is also on your side.

It is better to be patient than powerful; it is better to have self-control than to conquer a city.

PROVERBS 16:32 NLT

Ruling the Realm

If a man's home is his castle, how should he deal with the peasants who reside there with him? Whether it's living in a college dorm with other guys, staying in an apartment with a roommate, or abiding in your own house with a wife and kids, you'll often have to share your living space with others. Rubbing shoulders with the commoners every day can cause a great deal of friction, unless you take the Bible's advice and decide to be a little more forbearing than the average monarch.

The self-control needed to exercise patience with other people is different from the self-control it takes to manage anger. Patience is the all-important art of not becoming angry in the first place. It's about slowing down your response time, choosing not to make anger your knee-jerk reaction to every incident. This requires some will power, because it means resisting the natural inclination to get mad whenever someone steps on your toes. How do you do that? Ultimately, by relinquishing your "rights" as the master of your domain and counting yourself among the ordinary folk.

> **Patience, like wisdom, is a gift from God—and they go hand in hand.**

Patience, like wisdom, is a gift from God—and they go hand in hand. Understanding that God values other people's feelings just as much as he values yours will help you to cut your former royal subjects a little slack. Also, God can give you insight into others' points of view, enabling you to empathize with their perspectives and find ways to resolve conflict peacefully and without anger.

Ruling your realm with an iron fist may help you get your way, but it causes division in your relationships. Begin dealing with others patiently; it will bring harmony to your dwelling place.

Let us stop going over the basics of Christianity again and again. Let us go on instead and become mature in our understanding.

HEBREWS 6:1 NLT

Acorn to Oak

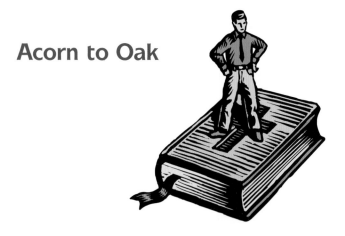

When a man is growing spiritually, his knowledge of God is increasing, his relationship with God is deepening, and his character is becoming more like God's. In the early stages, the change is amazing. He's like an acorn that becomes a sapling. Suddenly he has roots and a stem and leaves, and things are happening within him that he never could have imagined before. The question is, should he be satisfied with this dramatic transformation?

The writer of Hebrews said that the answer is no. An acorn is meant to develop all the way into an oak tree. God intends for a man to keep growing in his comprehension and experience until he is fully grown. An oak that's come of age produces new acorns, and a man reaches spiritual maturity when he has understood all the truths about God, has assimilated them into his life, and is able to teach them in a way that generates new faith in others.

> God intends for a man to keep growing in his comprehension and experience until he is fully grown.

You may be an acorn just becoming familiar with the foundational aspects of Christianity—things like repentance and faith and baptism and prayer. If so, focus on getting a solid grasp of these basics now so you'll be ready to keep growing once you've spread your leaves. On the other hand, you may be lingering in the sapling stage. In that case, find yourself a towering oak, a mature, godly man who can mentor you, challenging, encouraging, and inspiring you to keep reaching for the sky.

~⦿

Keep growing spiritually at every stage by continuing to trust God and obeying him. Respond positively to each new truth God reveals, and you'll move closer and closer to maturity.

Don't be afraid! Stand still and you will see the Lord save you today.

Exodus 14:13 ncv

Stand Tall

Some guys dream of building a boat and sailing around the world. If you ever actually try it, you're going to encounter adversity. Materials will break, things won't line up squarely, glue won't set properly. The hull will probably leak in at least one place. It's a fact of life that any worthwhile project will involve trouble. This world offers up all kinds of problems, and building a good boat requires a level of maturity and wisdom to overcome them. How much more so an ocean voyage.

The Bible clearly defines how a man should face adversity. Somehow people get the notion that life is supposed to be a pleasure cruise. The reality is that at times life is an arduous journey, fraught with misfortune and danger. It demands courage and fortitude. A boy could pilot a boat across the ocean if he faced nothing but blue skies and calm seas, but it takes a real man—relying

> **God has a purpose for you in this world—many purposes, in fact.**

on a real God—to negotiate turbulent waters and bring his vessel safely to port.

God has a purpose for you in this world—many purposes, in fact. Today you may have to tackle some tough financial issues at home. Tomorrow you may have to handle a crisis at work. The next day you may have to help family members resolve a difficult conflict. The wisdom and strength God offers will help you be the man he is calling you to be—and see you through every mission he has for you in life.

Anytime you face adversities in life, whether big or small, have courage, stick with it, and wait for God's help. He will sustain you through all of life's storms.

Be anxious for nothing, but in everything by prayer and supplication, with thanksgiving, let your requests be made known to God; and the peace of God, which surpasses all understanding, will guard your hearts and minds through Christ Jesus.

PHILIPPIANS 4:6–7 NKJV

Uncanny Calm

The Hebrew word for "peace," *shalom*, means more than mere serenity. It connotes a sense of wholeness and well-being. A man can experience this kind of peace even when his world's in turmoil and he's scrambling to put out fires. Living with God's peace is the opposite of living as many men do; rather than appearing okay on the outside and being torn up inside, you feel a deep calm within despite the chaos around you. Stress is responsible for many physical and emotional health problems men face, and God's peace will protect you from the ill effects of worrying.

If *shalom* doesn't describe your inner life, take a moment to pinpoint what you're concerned about. The apostle Paul said not to worry about anything. His advice seems hard to follow, but it's possible to stop agonizing over problems if you do something else instead. Replace your anxiety about the future with gratitude for all God's done for you in the past. Instead of trying to carry the weight of your cares, ask God to bear them for you.

> **Stress is responsible for many physical and emotional health problems men face, and God's peace will protect you from the ill effects of worrying.**

This takes a confidence in God that's rooted in knowledge of him and experience with him. Give God a chance to prove himself to you. It may not seem to make sense to walk away from your troubles emotionally, but after all, God's peace is a wonderful, inexplicable phenomenon.

~*~

Decide now to quit worrying about a specific concern, and ask God to replace your apprehension with his peace. Anytime you're tempted to worry about the situation again, choose to think about Paul's admonition instead.

Walk circumspectly, not as fools but as wise, redeeming the time.

EPHESIANS 5:15–16 NKJV

We are more than conquerors through Him who loved us.

ROMANS 8:37 NKJV

The Winner's Circle

The apostle Paul wrote that if God is on a man's side, that man will defeat whatever stands against him. By this he was referring to anything that tries to drive a wedge between a man and God. Paul insisted that God is too powerful, and his love is too great, to allow any situation to separate him from a man of faith. As long as such a man desires to keep up the fight, the struggle to stay close to God—though tough at times—is a battle he'll always win.

The devil wants to shatter your relationship with God. He will come at you with problems at work, difficulties at home, financial pressures, health issues, and even worries about world events, but he will never be able to separate God's love from you. There is a danger, however, that he could separate your love from God. Every relationship is a two-way street, after all. Maintaining your connection with God depends on whether you choose to stay on his side.

> **As long as such a man desires to keep up the fight, the struggle to stay close to God—though tough at times—is a battle he'll always win.**

That's what Paul meant in promising that you'll be triumphant through the one who cares most deeply about you. Keep returning God's love no matter what, so the bond between you will never be broken. When your relationship with God is intact and vibrant, with your love for each other flowing strongly both ways, there's nothing the two of you can't overcome. Remaining in the winner's circle with God is merely a function of your desire to be there.

∽◌

If you want to conquer your problems, make your relationship with God your number one concern, and ask God to address them with you. He will ensure your victory.

Let us run with endurance the race that is set before us.

Hebrews 12:1 NKJV

Tenacity

Men usually learn about perseverance when they're young. One way or another, a boy discovers that by keeping at it, he can complete a task that seems beyond him. Do you recall when you grasped this concept? You started a big project with a lot of enthusiasm, but soon reached a point when you thought you'd *never* be done. Yet through sheer will power, or because of your father's prodding, you pressed on—and eventually realized you were making real progress. Remember how great it felt to finish the job?

God often provides men with object lessons early in life to teach them principles they'll need later. This lesson about the value of tenacity is a prime example. God knows that if you're going to go the distance with him, living life his way, becoming everything he means you to be, accomplishing his purposes for you, and finally entering heaven, you've got to know what it means to stick with something and see it through to the end.

> **You've got to know what it means to stick with something and see it through to the end.**

The Bible speaks of a man's lifetime commitment to God as a race. Understanding that this race will demand persistence is critical to your success in running it well. There are going to come times of confusion when God won't make any sense to you, and times of uncertainty when you'll doubt that you can do all he requires of you. It's then that your steadfast determination to know God and obey him, coupled with encouragement and power from above, will carry you through.

It takes a never-say-die attitude to achieve eternal life. When you hit the wall in your marathon with God, remember the call to persevere. It will help you maintain your resolve.

$\mathbf{Y}$our attitude should be the same that
Christ Jesus had.

PHILIPPIANS 2:5 NLT

A Godly
Mind-Set

Perhaps lately you've decided you could use a little attitude adjustment. You may have reached this conclusion on
your own, or some significant person in your life may have
pointed it out to you. But short of whacking yourself in the
head with a tire iron, what can you do about it? The Bible
has some simple yet profound answers to this dilemma, and
it all begins with this straightforward, powerful verse.

So what was Jesus's attitude? Interestingly enough, the
word *attitude* has another meaning besides state of mind. It
also indicates position in relation to a reference point. Jesus
was always in perfect alignment with God, which means he

always maintained a proper mind-set. He was in perfect synch with his heavenly Father. Therefore Jesus was also right in tune with God's Spirit and with all of God's laws written in the Bible. Not a bad approach to life.

The best way to describe Jesus's mind-set is to say that his mind was set on heavenly things—which is exactly where the Bible recommends you fix your thoughts. Scripture warns against the natural inclination

> **The Bible offers an intriguing proposition: a transformation of the mind, a renewed way of thinking.**

to focus on yourself and on material things. Instead, the Bible offers an intriguing proposition: a transformation of the mind, a renewed way of thinking. Not just an attitude adjustment but a complete attitude overhaul. The payoff for embracing Jesus's attitude is that, like him, you'll squarely align yourself with God's perfect will for your life.

Nobody likes being hit over the head with a Bible, but it beats a two-by-four. Jesus was intimately acquainted with God's Word; fill your mind with the Bible's truths, and God will transform your attitude.

Forgive one another as quickly and thoroughly as God in Christ forgave you.

EPHESIANS 4:32 MSG

Forgiveness: Wherefores and Whys

Your business partner left the company, taking with him some of your most important clients by undermining their confidence in you. Bitter, your God-given sense of justice offended, you're considering how to respond. Now is when a solid understanding of what the Bible says about forgiveness becomes crucial. The apostle Paul didn't pussyfoot around; he stated the truth plainly. While you ponder whether to forgive or not, it is crystal clear that there's no option. God commands you to forgive.

Paul divulged the hows and whys of forgiveness. They are simply put. How soon are you to forgive? Quickly, immediately. To what extent are you to forgive? Thoroughly, completely. Why are you to forgive? Because God forgave you.

One powerful phrase that Paul used reveals the miracle that made it possible for God to forgive your sins and lovingly embrace you. That miracle enables you to forgive others as well. How can forgiveness happen? "In Christ." When Jesus died on the cross, a great paradox was resolved. At the cross, God's sense of

> While you ponder whether to forgive or not, it is crystal clear that there's no option. God commands you to forgive.

justice was satisfied: in Christ he took the punishment for your sins. At the cross, God's sense of mercy was also satisfied: in Christ he forgave you. The cross is where justice and mercy, two diametrically opposed concepts, intersect. It's where God chose to deal with your sins, and it's where he wants you to deal with the sins of others.

Has someone wronged you? Obey God and forgive that individual, relinquishing the right to convict him or her, choose a punishment, and deliver it. Release the person into the merciful and just hands of God.

Imitate me, just as I also imitate Christ.

1 CORINTHIANS 11:1 NKJV

Chain of Command

To lead others effectively, a man must have a firm idea of where he's taking them, and a deep conviction that the destination is worth striving for. Often, being a good leader also requires a man to be a good follower, to fall in behind someone of even greater vision and authority. This was all true for the apostle Paul, a powerful leader who spearheaded the spread of Christianity from Jerusalem to Rome. In his case, the person he was following and the goal he was directing others toward were the same: Jesus.

Jesus himself was both a leader and a follower. He started a world religion, understanding exactly where he was taking his disciples and knowing firsthand how worthy the object of their journey was. At the same time, he was in constant contact with God, whom he listened to and obeyed completely. Just as with Paul, the one Jesus was following and the goal he was guiding people toward were identical.

> **Jesus himself was both a leader and a follower.**

You can read all about Paul's life and teachings in the Bible; he wrote much of the New Testament. If you take up his lead, doing as he says and does, he'll bring you right to Jesus. And as you follow Jesus, obeying his instructions and emulating his deeds, he will take you straight to God. Paul's writings form the first link in a critical chain of command that you need to join, for your own sake and for the sake of those who are following you.

—

People will follow your lead. Especially if you're a father, pay attention to your actions as well as your words. Others will always place more emphasis on what you do than on what you say.

Do not let loyalty and faithfulness forsake you; bind them around your neck, write them on the tablet of your heart. So you will find favor and good repute in the sight of God and of people.

PROVERBS 3:3–4 NRSV

A True Man

Why are men drawn to war movies? What is it about films that revolve around battle, whether it's ancient conflict, modern combat, or even fantasy warfare as in *The Lord of the Rings*? Surely action and adventure play a role. But more compelling than all the explosions and derring-do is the element of heroism, self-sacrifice, and loyalty that constitutes the real glory of war.

Humankind is in an epic battle against evil, and steadfast devotion is the secret to fighting well, winning the victory, and earning great renown. By committing yourself to

God, to people, and to causes greater than yourself, and by making loyalty an integral part of your character, you'll become a true man, a real hero. God and others will hold you in high esteem—and deep down, in a healthy way that's unrelated to false pride, you'll think more highly of yourself as well.

A warrior of old would often carry the token of a loved one into battle, perhaps wearing a chain and pendant around his neck or tying a scarf on his arm. In many ways the practice persists with soldiers today. Find some way to remind yourself on a daily basis of your commitment to God and to the people in your life. Set your heart on upholding your allegiances. Life isn't easy, and at times it will be tempting to give up the fight and run, but if you remain dedicated to God and others, you will earn their highest praise.

> **Humankind is in an epic battle against evil, and steadfast devotion is the secret to fighting well.**

Faithfulness is a gift from above; like all godly character traits, you can't form it in your heart on your own. Begin asking God each day to help you develop it.

$\mathbf{Y}$ou have been saved by grace through believing. You did not save yourselves; it was a gift from God.

EPHESIANS 2:8 NCV

A Priceless Gift

When some thrill-seeking sailor gets himself in trouble by venturing into dangerous conditions out on the Atlantic Ocean, the Coast Guard quickly mobilizes to make a rescue. It's a costly proposition, and recently there's been talk of requiring the person who needs assistance to foot the bill. But for now salvation by helicopter from a stormy sea remains a free service—an expensive and valuable gift, so to speak.

God's salvation from hell is also free of charge. He offers it to you by grace, which simply means he's giving you something very good that you haven't earned. The fact is, like the foolish sailor, you've made wrong choices that have landed you in a dire predicament. By all objective measures, you deserve the fate that awaits you. But because God loves you so much, he is willing to pay the ultimate price to rescue you. (That's the definition of *mercy*, by the way—God's preventing you from experiencing something very bad that you *have* earned.)

So now you're hanging on for dear life on the deck of your battered sailboat. The wind is howling and the waves are threatening to wash you overboard. Suddenly you hear a chopper overhead and see a lifeline

> **Faith is grabbing hold of the lifeline that God has lovingly, graciously, and mercifully gone to such great lengths to provide you.**

dropping toward you. At this point you have a choice. Will you entrust your life to the boat or to the helicopter? Faith is grabbing hold of the lifeline that God has lovingly, graciously, and mercifully gone to such great lengths to provide you.

—⁂—

Will you trust in Jesus, whom God sacrificed to pay for his mission to rescue you? God's gift is priceless, and it's dangling right in front of you. It's faith in Jesus that saves your life forever.

I am the way, the truth, and the life.

JOHN 14:6 NKJV

Ultimate Reality

Men often wrestle with questions about the meaning of life. They need meaning in their lives, to give them hope and the strength to carry on. Sometimes they rack their brains trying to figure out what life is all about. But once they accept that God exists, they begin to understand that Jesus is the reason they're living, and then the universe begins to make sense. Jesus is the linchpin that holds everything together.

There are two important, related reasons why you need to know that Jesus is the be-all and end-all of existence. First, if your life is going to be successful in any meaningful sense of the word, you have to know which end is up.

Recognizing that Jesus is the beginning and the end of all there is in life gives you the layout of the land. Everything else flows from that basic fact. Building your life on that key premise will prevent you from basing it on a lie.

> **Recognizing that Jesus is the beginning and the end of all there is in life gives you the layout of the land.**

Second, once you realize that Jesus is the essence of all truth, you'll know whom to believe. Over and over Jesus said, in essence, "Here's the fact of the matter . . ." Then he went on to relate a powerful principle. If you've already resolved Jesus's identity in your mind, you won't have to struggle over whether to follow his teachings or not. You'll be poised to act quickly on them. You'll be positioned for ultimate success.

—⁂

Make Jesus the center of your existence. Then you can live out your life with a sense of confidence and peace, knowing that there really is a purpose to it all.

Husbands, love your wives, just as Christ also loved the church and gave Himself for her.

EPHESIANS 5:25 NKJV

Giving Your All

The Bible portrays Jesus's relationship to the "church," which consists of all the people in the world who love him and have joined their lives to his, as a marriage. Jesus is the groom and his followers, taken as a whole, are his bride. It must be easier for women to see themselves in the latter role in this picture, but the metaphor conveys a profound truth for all, one the apostle Paul described as a great mystery. However, Paul also used the analogy in a way that men can more readily relate to, in describing their responsibility as husbands.

Jesus demonstrated the depth of his love for his bride through his willingness to die to rescue her. He showed that he is the type of groom who would throw himself in front of a speeding car to save the one he loves. In holding up Jesus as an example for husbands, Paul was saying that even if God doesn't call on you to love your wife just as dramatically, he intends for you to love her just as much.

> **Prove to your bride the extent of your devotion by serving her, bearing with her faults, and being kind and compassionate toward her.**

Paul's point was that loving a woman is more than cherishing her. Prove to your bride the extent of your devotion by serving her, bearing with her faults, and being kind and compassionate toward her. Give her encouragement and respect. Look after her and protect her, talk to her honestly, and always be gentle with her feelings. Giving your all, as Jesus did, is every groom's duty and joy.

Are you loving your bride as much as Jesus does his? Doing so will touch her deeply. Just as people respond to Jesus because of his selfless love for them, your wife will draw closer to you.

All of you must yield to the government rulers. No one rules unless God has given him the power to rule, and no one rules now without that power from God.

ROMANS 13:1 NCV

The Powers That Be

There are two types of dominion in a man's life, the power he exerts over others and the command others hold over him. The essential thing to remember about both is that God always establishes the powers that be. When you're in control, this truth will give you confidence; you'll know that as God's chosen man, you can depend on him for wisdom and guidance. It will also keep you humble, because you'll recognize that only God deserves credit for your rise to prominence. He placed you in your position of influence, and you'll need his approval and help to stay there.

When you must submit to another, knowing that God assigns all authority will give you peace of mind. You'll realize that since God is in control, it's right for you to obey whomever he puts over you, so long as you're not ordered to do anything immoral. If God places you under the authority of someone ungodly, remember Joseph, the favored son of Jacob,

> **No matter where you rank in this world, you'll always be serving God.**

who was sold by his brothers into slavery in Egypt and spent the rest of his life under pagan rule. He trusted God and served his masters faithfully, and the Lord was with him, made him successful, and used him powerfully.

No matter where you rank in this world, you'll always be serving God. Believe in his sovereignty, rule over others with humility and integrity, submit to whatever authority God puts over you, and he'll reward you with a life of significance and accomplishment.

"Freedom in Christ" doesn't allow you to flout the authority God has placed you under. Use your freedom instead to please God by choosing to obey him through your compliance with the authority of those above you.

Rejoice always, pray without ceasing, in everything give thanks; for this is the will of God in Christ Jesus for you.

1 Thessalonians 5:16–18 nkjv

Eternal Gratitude

Developing a grateful heart isn't a matter of white-washing your life with a thin coat of paint, trying to fool yourself into thinking that everything's bright and cheery. It's more like inviting an appraiser from *The Antiques Roadshow* to move into your home and keep reminding you just how valuable all the stuff in your life really is. It's fostering a deep appreciation for all the good things God has given you.

Expressing your gratitude to God every day is a vital part of cultivating your relationship with him. What a difference it makes to a father when his son keeps telling him thanks. Your constant awareness of God's blessings will draw you closer to him, and your sincere words of recognition for everything he has done will draw him closer to you. Practicing continual gratefulness leads to greater intimacy with God.

Gratitude also leads to greater happiness, and that's exactly God's plan for you. His desire is for you to be joyful all the time. He wants you to

> **Practicing continual gratefulness leads to greater intimacy with God.**

keep the lines of communication with him open, living every moment with a sense of genuine appreciation that overflows into your prayers. This isn't about having a perfect life; you can experience all these aspects of a close, loving relationship with God despite the problems men often encounter, such as job pressures, financial struggles, health concerns, and relational difficulties. The difference is that you face every trouble with a song in your heart, one of thankfulness and joy.

Practice gratefulness by spending time thanking God whenever you pray, before making any requests. Consider all you have to be thankful for, and ask God to develop in you a constant attitude of appreciation.

This hope we have as an anchor of the soul, both sure and steadfast.

HEBREWS 6:19 NKJV

Sure Thing

Every man needs hope to go on living, to get out of bed in the morning. But there has to be something more to it than pie-in-the-sky dreams and wishful thinking. It's got to be more substantial than some mere emotion. What a man needs to sustain him through the turbulence of life is the assurance that there's a bright future in store for him. And this is exactly the kind of hope that God offers.

True hope is a rock-solid certainty. Let go of tenuous prospects and grab hold of the real thing. There is stability in the hope God brings a man. It inspires a deep conviction that every expectation will be fulfilled. That's because true hope is anchored in the bedrock knowledge that God has the future under his control.

With true hope comes a steady and growing sense of joy. When you accept the hope God extends to you, the rest of your life begins to feel like the last few seconds of a blowout Super Bowl game. There's still time on the clock, but thanks to your brilliant coach, the outcome has already been decided. A

> What a man needs to sustain him through the turbulence of life is the assurance that there's a bright future in store for him.

great victory is in the bag. Soon your team will begin to enjoy all the fruit of success. And even though you and your teammates have to finish the game, you can't help but start celebrating early.

in the hope you're clinging to provide a stable mooring for your spirit? If not, abandon it and reach for true hope. The hope God offers will always bring you peace and joy.

The one who rejects you, rejects me. And rejecting me is the same as rejecting God, who sent me.

LUKE 10:16 MSG

Divine Solidarity

Men in creative fields such as advertising or design learn not to take it personally when something they've produced isn't accepted by a boss or a client. They look at it merely as a negation of their efforts, not of them. God sees things a little differently, though. When somebody writes off a guy who's trying to live for him, God identifies very closely with the man he worked hard to create. God takes it to heart anytime you're discarded because of him.

Jesus was dismissed by the majority of people eventually, and he warned his closest followers that they'd be treated the same way. But he also expressed his solidarity with them, and God's as well. Jesus was not only saying that any rejection they experienced represented a refusal of him and God; he was also promising that both he and his heavenly Father would stand beside them through thick and thin.

> **God takes it to heart anytime you're discarded because of him.**

If you're a man dedicated to living your life for God, you're bound to take it personally when someone you care about turns away from you because of your beliefs. How can you not, when following Jesus has become such an integral part of who you are? You're sure to feel forsaken and sad. You'll never go through such rejection alone, however, because Jesus and God are right there at your side. They've been through it all before, and they've sworn never to abandon you.

—

Pray for those who judge you negatively. That's what Jesus did. There's always hope that a person who rejects you because of your faith in Jesus will one day embrace you for the same reason.

God is our refuge and strength, a very present help in trouble.

PSALM 46:1 NKJV

Crisis Team

The best way to handle a crisis is to rely on a team of persons who have gone through an intensive training regimen and bonded into a cohesive, highly effective unit. The members are practiced, recognize their individual roles and how they fit into the group effort, and know they can trust their teammates to perform under pressure.

Disaster recovery groups, hospitals, and military organizations have learned the wisdom of this team-based method of crisis management. The Bible teaches that it's an approach every man needs to adopt. Whatever difficulties you may experience in life—in your career, your relationships, your finances, your health—you don't have to face them alone. God is ready to respond with you to any situation that arises.

The key component of any crisis team is the loyalty among its members. Military leaders know that a unit of soldiers who train together will be more effective than a group who train separately, because of this loyalty. God is already completely devoted to you, and he knows his job.

> **The key component of any crisis team is the loyalty among its members.**

Commit to learning more about God and your job as part of his team. You'll find that when difficult times come, you'll be instinctively aware that God is with you, you'll know both your role and his in a crisis, and you'll have no doubt that you can rely on him.

The challenge for you is to enter into a lifelong training process with God now, before things heat up. Draw up a crisis-preparedness plan that includes studying the Bible, praying, and inviting God to help you deal with everyday issues.

Let us think about each other and help each other to show love and do good deeds. You should not stay away from the church meetings, as some are doing, but you should meet together and encourage each other.

HEBREWS 10:24–25 NCV

Family Time

In the movie *Apollo 13*, astronaut Jim Lovell (played by Tom Hanks) has an interesting shift of perspective. At first he's fiercely intent on going to the moon. It's his dream, his purpose in life. Later, orbiting the moon in a badly damaged spacecraft, unable to descend to the surface, Lovell sees the earth rise over the horizon. Suddenly he adopts a new mission, and becomes single-mindedly focused on getting home to his family.

Similarly, men today need to experience a radical shift in thinking about church. Instead of dismissing church as irrelevant and either avoiding it completely or just putting in time once a week before concentrating on other matters, men have to recognize that developing their relationship with God and with others *is* the essential thing in life. Jesus stated very clearly that the Bible's two most important commands are to love God and to love people. And the primary way God instituted for you to fulfill this mission is through involvement with a local church.

> **Men today need to experience a radical shift in thinking about church.**

A church is not merely a building, and it's not just a weekly gathering of individuals; it's all about getting connected with a community, becoming a member of a family. Joining and participating in a local church fulfills a deeply felt need for men in today's world: the need to escape isolation and insignificance by forming meaningful relationships with both their Creator and other people. It deals with the heart of the matter, and there's nothing more relevant than that.

~*/||○

Many churches try hard to ensure that the message they share and the community life they provide are relevant to men today. Are you making an effort to find a church that's right for you?

You are worthy, O Lord, to receive glory and honor and power; for You created all things, and by Your will they exist and were created.

REVELATION 4:11 NKJV

Reason for Praise

Think of the admiration and praise heaped on famous men, guys who are artists, composers, authors, architects, engineers. They're lauded immensely for their creations, yet all of their accomplishments together don't begin to compare with God's.

If all God had ever done was to make the universe and set life into motion, a man would have all the reason he needs to worship him forever. God would deserve your highest adulation even if he had only made the world, folded his arms, and watched what happened. But he has done much more. He has been intimately involved with humankind since the very beginning, and continues to be. The Bible tells many stories of his great acts in ancient days. History is full of accounts of his amazing deeds since then. And today countless men can tell of the marvelous things God has done for them. You may be one such man.

> **If all God had ever done was to make the universe and set life into motion, a man would have all the reason he needs to worship him forever.**

The story's not over yet; God is not nearly finished with all he intends to do. The Bible promises he will create a new earth someday, a world far more glorious than this one. So regardless of your circumstances or how you feel at any given moment—whether you're paddling a canoe downriver on a sunny afternoon or scraping your knuckles trying to change a flat tire in the rain—there is always good cause for you to praise God. He is worthy of it for all he has done, all he is doing, and all he will do.

Seek to understand God's loving nature, and picture each moment of your life in the context of all his awesome deeds. Always remember God's goodness, and continually offer him your adoration and worship.

Every promise of the LORD your God has come true. Not a single one has failed!

JOSHUA 23:14 NLT